THROUGH GOD...

Bought, Brought, and Broke Through

Jimmy Rush

Measure of Faith Books

THROUGH GOD…
BOUGHT, BROUGHT, AND BROKE THROUGH
by Jimmy Rush

Copyright © 2018 Jimmy Rush

Published by
Measure of Faith Books
PO Box 6122
Fort Hood, TX 76544

All rights reserved.

No part of this publication may be reproduced or transmitted in any form or by any means, electronic, mechanical, including photocopying, or by any information storage and retrieval system, without written permission from the author, except for the inclusion of a brief quotations in a review.

ISBN 978-0-692-16235-4 (softcover)
ISBN 978-0-692-15098-6 (hardcover)
ISBN 978-1-5323-8159-1 (eBook)

Library of Congress Control Number: 2018908271

DISCLAIMER: The information reflected within this book are the author's personal thoughts and beliefs. These thoughts and beliefs do not necessarily represents the views of Department of Defense, United States Army, or its components.

First Edition 2018

Printed in the United States of America

Contents

Introduction 1

Poem: My Struggle Through 2

I. **Through God, I Was Bought with the the Blood of Jesus (The Waters of Purpose)** .. 6

1: Into the Garden 7
2: Exiting the Garden 19
3: Rising Waters: The Blood of Protection 27
4: Special Recruit for the Kingdom 35

II. **God Brought Me Through the World System (The Rivers Plans)** 40

5: Rivers with No Remorse 41
6: Psalm 23: Searching for Still Waters 47

Poem: A Story in a Not So Perfect Life 50

7: Finishing What God Started 53
8: God Taught Me How to Hold a Tune 59
9: Favor from the Savior 66
10: Your Identity and Truth Are in the Blood ... 72
11: Rivers of Rejection through God 79

III. Broke Through My Hurt, Habit, and Hang-ups (The Fires of Promise) 90

12: Choose This Day Friend or Foe 91
13: Through the Fire: Don't Stop, Drop, or Roll 97
14: Formed by Fire 103
15: Breaking Through Fire of Fear 108
16: Battle Tested for Breakthrough 114
17: Refiners Fire 120
18: Don't Forget to Say Thanks 126

Poem: Cannot Thank You Enough 129

19: Promise Keeper: No Scorches or Burns 135
20: Not Yet…Just Getting Started 143

Conclusion 151
Acknowledgments 157
About the Author 161

Introduction

SUPPORTIVE SCRIPTURE: Isaiah 43:2 "When you pass through the waters, I will be with you; And through the rivers, they will not overtake you, When you walk through the fire, you will not be scorched, Nor will the flame burn you."

Living by example, and not just giving lip service is something that has become a way of life. We have learned how to be grateful for both times of lack and times of plenty. For every soul God places in our paths, we want to ensure when they leave our presence they have felt the presence of God, and all glory and honor points back to Him.

We have learned what it means to allow God to be our refuge, because through God is where our strength is complete, our joy is everlasting, and our peace is secured. We have come to know God for ourselves and built our foundation on him.

Jimmy and LeTasha Rush

My Struggle Through

As I sit in this unorganized little world of mine,
I ask the question. How hard can it get? Does the
world have to revolve around lies and tricks?
Everything I pretty much want I get, except that
thing called love which I long and destined for.
People are filling my head up with all that witchcraft
and voodoo. Why can't they just understand?
My struggle and what I am going through.

Now people say how a person like you was
struggling when you have everything you want.
I just hang my head in sorrow knowing all along
I don't.

Am I too blind that I cannot see love or is it
everything I see becoming unreal to me or a blur?
All I wanted was for the excellent time to roll, stop
feeling sorry for myself and stop feeling blue.
Maybe one day they'll see My Struggle Through.

How can I stop the pain? Will this so-called love
drive me insane? Will this person step up and
realize I'm so simple and laid out so plain?

There are a lot of things I can do, but who's fooling who. Everything I'm saying is right. Open your eyes and realize My Struggle Through.

This is the first poem that I wrote at the age of fifteen. Poetry was my outlet, the way I expressed myself, and my therapy for depression and pain.

My life over the last thirty-nine years has been full of lessons. Some of those lessons were taught to me by way of trials (The Waters of Purpose), tribulations (The Rivers of Plans), and disappointment (The Fires of Promise). All the lessons have brought me great success and experience. During those lessons, I have been privileged enough to have been taught by some of the most significant examples that God could have placed on this earth. Journey with me through the waters, the rivers, and fires that God brought me through, the promises that God brought me through, and the barriers I had to break through to get God's purpose fulfilled through my life.

My journey through all the processes is making me who I am today and will become in the future. Some of the most significant lessons that I have learned and experienced were not from my success but from my failures. In those moments of failure, I realized that there are some lessons in life that I had to learn to gain the experience needed to deal with the next test.

One of my favorite things to do in my youth was to write poetry. My poetry was used to express and encourage myself and those whom the poems were written for. Throughout this book, you will read several poems written by me from the place in my life where I was hurting the most. Isaiah penned Isaiah 43:2 especially for me when he said, "When you pass through the waters, I will be with you."

Life as I knew it from the 1980s, up to 2010 growing up consisted of decades of troubling waters that I had to pass through. Some waters were shallow, deep, dirty, or troublesome. Other waters were polluted and caused more damage than it was helping. I needed a fresh drink of water, the very same drink that was offered to the woman of Samaria in John 4:13–14. Maybe I just needed to be led beside the still water that David was in Psalm 23:2. There was a longing for a place of certainty and protection while going through the rivers.

The rivers that I had to face were moving rapidly and violently. I needed some stability in my life, and

I needed to settle down. What I wouldn't give to be that tree planted by the rivers of water so that when my season came, I could bring forth the fruit as is described in Psalm 1:3. I wanted to discover personally for myself the river described in Psalm 46:4: "There is a river, the streams whereof shall make glad the city of God, the holy place of the tabernacles of the Highest."

The first problem with going through the waters and rivers is that when it was time for me to go through the fire, there was nothing to quench the fire. I am incredibly grateful that my walk through the fire came at an early age. While going through the fire, I was scared and, at times, stranded, but never scorched. There were times when I was battered, bruised, and, yes, broken, but never burned. God has held true to His word. My sole desire is to do the will of the one who sent me, to be the beloved son to the father, for God to speak boldly about me like John recorded and said that I too am the disciple that Jesus loved.

I. Through God, I Was Bought with the Blood of Jesus (The Waters of Purpose)

1

Into the Garden

The word mess is defined as a situation or state of affairs that is confused or full of difficulties. Folks, when I tell you my life was a mess, I needed some guidance, purpose, and a plan.

I grew up in Mount Zion Garden Apartments, which were projects located in Albany, Georgia. My mom Memory was a single parent raising four kids, all from different fathers. She was raising up three girls, Tabatha, Tonya, and Tamara, and me being the second oldest and the only boy, Johnny Lee Journey Jr. We lived off government assistance, hand-me-downs, and any other way that God saw fit to supply all of our needs. I could only imagine the impact and burden of trying to raise four kids on your own.

It was not long before the tests and trials of life began to weigh heavily on the family. Those tests and trials came in the form of crack cocaine and attached itself to our mom. We were now vulnerable to attacks from all directions. It started with days with no food, no lights, and no hot water, and foster care soon followed. There were times when some of my friends and I would spend all day jumping in and out of a dumpster to collect aluminum cans to turn in to one of the older ladies in the projects for food and, on a good day, cash. My mom started spending time in jail and prison for a variety of reasons, none that I knew the charges. Several other things attached themselves to my three siblings and me, some of which are their stories and theirs alone to tell.

My grandmother Georgia Mae South stepped in to care for us so that we were not placed in the care of the state. We had more liberty with my grandmother than we did with my mother. Some of my friends and I started coming up with crazy games to play.

One of those games was throwing rocks at cars, which got me arrested and placed on probation for six months. I spent my Saturdays raking a yard full of pine straw for some nuns at a church, who rewarded me with a pastry after about four to five hours of work. Not to mention I had to catch the bus once a month downtown to see my probation officer and pay my fine. All of this was before the age of ten. I was exposed to so much before the age of ten including pornography and sex.

I failed the second grade, and it was not due to bad grades. It was because of my inability at that time to pronounce certain words that begin with the letter S, and I had no one to intervene on my behalf at that time. We rarely missed days out of school, because that was our source of food. I can remember one of my goals was to get perfect attendance just to get a certificate at the end of the year.

Two of my sisters and I spent time in different foster homes. The smell of spoiled meat and loneliness still plague me to this day, and we were grateful that we never had to be separated. So whatever people deemed necessary for our lives they pretty much did, besides all the odds were stacked against us.

Something great came out of my failing the second grade, and that was my second grade teacher Mrs. Wendy Grace. Although she had a classroom full of kids, she had a gift for making each person feel special. I certainly felt special whenever I entered her class. One thing that did not matter to her was the fact I was a poor African American boy, and she was Caucasian in a time when prejudice and racism were very much apparent. She was indeed a visible blessing from God and a reminder that He was a present help through her in the time of need. I was missing something, and searching for that something was not going to be an easy task.

One of the most significant questions that I used to ask my mom was, "Why didn't my dad ever come to see me? Did I do something wrong? Am I a bad kid and is that why my dad did not want to know me?"

These questions all seemed to pop up when I was upset with my mom or wanted an item that my mom was unable to afford during that time. I used to spend some time with my dad's mom whom I called Grandmother Pearl Journey and stepbrother Justin before we moved to Mount Zion. I remember my Aunt Joy, my cousins Ron and Daniel, and we shared fantastic times together.

My dad was in the military, so he was often gone. One of the hardest times for me in school was show-and-tell. The teacher would go around the classroom, and everyone would talk about how great their dad was or show some item that fascinated the class. When my turn came around, I had nothing to share but that my dad was in the military, which the class seemed to enjoy. But I knew little of him and what branch of the military he was a part of at the time. So moving to Mount Zion that contact was broken, for some reason unknown to me. Those moments and people are critical and later on in the book you will see why. My mom always had a way of assuring me that she was doing the best she could and things would get better.

There was a time in Mount Zion Garden that three out of the five of my grandmother's children stayed in the projects at one time. My mom, Uncle Jared and his wife Jewel, and Uncle Ant. So as the only boy, I had the luxury of bouncing from house to house.

My Uncle Ant was the youngest, and he made sure that I had essential things as a young boy such as shoes, clothes, and street knowledge. He was serious about family and was well respected in Albany. I spent most of my time at my Uncle Jared and Aunt Jewel's apartment, and they had two kids, Caleb and Joshua. My Uncle Jared and his family always made sure that they saved room for me. Caleb, Joshua, and I were practically inseparable. I treated them more like brothers than cousins. I was very protective of those two boys, and they seemed to enjoy having me around. I was always glad to be in their company. They brought a lot of attention from all around the projects. They were well mannered, and people thought they were twins, Aunt Jewel assured they were well dressed and not to mention they were incredibly handsome young men. My Uncle Jade was serving overseas in the military, so he was gone much of the time. My Aunt Diamond had moved to Gary, Indiana, along with her four kids.

Another neat thing that happens while staying in the projects was people from all walks of life moved out there. The Rome family (Aunt Glow, and her four sons, Kenneth, Kelvin, Keith, and Kane) moved to Mount Zion Garden, and I later found out we were related.

Before I tell how unique that family is to me, I have to let you in on one of my character flaws. I was a very timid boy until the Rome moved to the projects. I used to get picked on and bullied, and I would run from fights. Not only did I run from fights, and I would stop running toward fights. There was a fight in the front of the projects taking place with some older kids. In a family, whenever a fight took place, everyone would run toward the fight. This particular day I did not have to run to the fight, I was there when it was initiated. In the midst of the fight, one of the ladies picked up a stick and threw it at the person involved in the fight, and she missed her desired target by a mile. But that stick met me dead in the lips and split both my top and bottom lips leaving me with big lips—a physical characteristic that I used to be so ashamed and self-conscious about.

From that day on if I was not personally running from fights, I was running away from the ones that did not involve me. My oldest sister, Tabatha, fought most of my battles. I was one of the fastest and strongest kids in the projects but the scariest.

The Rome were very athletic, well mannered, and they accepted me. My cousin (Keith) made me fight back, made me believe in myself, and let me know that I was stronger than other kids and taught me how to use my strength. Later on, we found out that my dad, Johnny Senior's mom, the late Pearl Journey, and my Aunt Glow were sisters.

Another thing that made the Rome's special to me was the fact that I almost drowned three times, and two out of the three times I was saved by one of the

Rome brothers—once by Kenneth and once by Kelvin. I indeed owed God more gratitude and thanks for allowing that family into my life. That was confirmation to me that family structure was essential to God.

One thing I can tell you about my family, they were God-fearing. We said grace before every meal and prayer before going to bed. We only knew one grace, and that was, "God is great, God is good, let us thank Him for our food. Bow our heads, we are fed, give us Lord our daily bread. Amen." Our one prayer at night was, "Now I lay me down to sleep, I pray the Lord my soul to keep. If I die before I wake, I pray the Lord, my soul to take. Amen."

But that is all I knew about God. It did not help that my great-grandfather (Will Silk) was a preacher in Dawson, Georgia, and I had never heard him preach. One of my favorite childhood memories was when we used to travel to visit our great-grandparents the late Rev. Will Silk and First Lady Katie Silk aka Madea house located in Dawson, Georgia, for the Fourth of July celebration. Albany to Dawson was less than thirty miles, but for a child, it seems like it took an eternity to get there.

The event was an organized red-carpet affair all combined in one extraordinary moment. My great-grandparents had a total of thirteen children, and everyone from that thirteen had multiple children. The excitement about going to our great-grandparents' house was spending time with uncles, aunts, and cousins, and we did our best to dress to impress. We waited around to see who had the sharpest car, latest shoes, and the newest addition to the family.

After the red-carpet affair was over, we would help ourselves to some peaches, plums, figs, and sugar canes. My great-grandfather was always the center of attraction and a great cook. My great-grandmother kept things in order and ensured that everyone got along.

Another summer highlight was when we traveled to Parrot, Georgia, which was a little less than seven miles from Dawson. On my mother's paternal side, her father's brother stayed on a farm with his wife and five kids. When the four of us and the five of them met, we were unrestrained with no restrictions, because it was the country with plenty of open space for kids to enjoy themselves.

No matter the location or who was around, my family ensured that we made God the center of attention. It seemed as if time was moving fast, and I was passing through some fast-rising water and needed a Savior to give me purpose. I can remember the different religious groups knocking on the door and giving us bible studies. I also remember a bus would come pick us up to go to church, but we were only interested in going to church on specific Sundays because the church served food. One thing I was focused on as a kid was the way the preacher would tell a story of the bible and get passionate about what he was preaching. The preachers would beat their hands on the pulpit while wiping their mouths and faces with their cloths. I perceived those sermons as good stories, uplifting even as a young kid, but they remained a parable to me.

Without a confession of the Lord Jesus as my Lord and Savior, those sermons would remain a good story. As a young boy, one thing I would get in trouble for the most was not taking a bath. I hated taking a bath. My life was in desperate need of a different type of washing. I needed to be washed in the blood of Jesus Christ. Even at the age of ten, being washed in blood seemed a little extreme.

God was doing some excellent things for me so that being washed in the blood was a small drop in the bucket. Without a confession and without being washed in the blood, I was never going to be redeemed.

I can remember being a ten-year-old child suffering from asthma attacks and eczema, wondering what I did to deserve this life with these disabilities. Wondering if these things would be the death of me. Not to mention the numerous times I questioned God as to how much time I had on earth and how short life was. I just wanted the ability to hold up a sword like He-Man and call on the power of Grayskull, or call on some friends like Thunder Cats and perhaps a car like Kid in Night Rider. It was just my ten-year-old imagination running wild.

What was so special about this man called Jesus that my great-grandfather preached about, and to whom my grandmother and mom also prayed? If none of what I was going through wasn't my fault or my parents' faults, then why did I need to be redeemed? All I needed was God to push the restart button on my life. I was reminded of John 9:1–3. When Jesus passed a man who was blind at birth, His disciples asked Jesus who sinned: the man or his parents. The disciple had perceived that since the boy was blind, someone had to have sinned. That is the same feeling that I was having as a young boy. I felt I either did something wrong, or my mom or dad had. "Jesus answered, it was not this man or his parents sinned, but he was born blind so that the workings of God should be manifested (displayed and illustrated) in him." God was doing a work in me for Him to be put on display.

With several turns of events, we had to leave the projects, and my world as I knew it was about to come to an end—having to leave my friends, the playground, and not to mention the place I called home. Roman 5:8 stated, "But God demonstrates his love for us in this: While we were still sinners, Christ died for us." God did not wait for me or my environment to get itself together before He sent His son Jesus to save us. Jesus bought my purpose with his life even while I was sinning.

2

Exiting the Garden

We moved out of the projects of Mount Zion Garden with our grandmother after our mother admitted herself into a rehabilitation center.

We moved to Hickory Lane, a place for the five of us in a two-bedroom apartment—my grandmother and the four of us. My grandmother had five children: Diamond, the late Jared South, Jade, Ant, and my mother Memory. My aunt moved back to Georgia from Indiana. Diamond had three boys and one girl, and my mother had three girls and one boy. So when we moved to Hickory Lane with my grandmother, I spent much of my time with my Aunt Diamond with her three boys.

My cousin Jose was my Aunt Diamond's oldest son. Jose and I were inseparable. We did everything together and shared everything. He certainly played the big brother role, and on many occasions, he kept me from getting picked on and bullied at school.

Like I mentioned earlier we did not have much, but Jose would loan me clothes and shoes, and we would switch clothes and shoes to keep from getting put to shame. Jose had a pretty good reputation. Therefore, I never had to worry about fighting too much. We spent most of our time playing sandlot football, throw-em up bust-em up, and wrestling matches. If we were not playing an outdoor sport, we spent time playing Nintendo, and our favorite was chasing girls.

One of the reasons that I enjoyed staying with my Aunt Diamond was she had fun with her kids, and she always made room for me and called me her chocolate baby. She also stayed next door to the late Darling Rose. Mrs. Rose had a granddaughter by the name of Aaliya Bond (Liya) who stayed with her frequently. When I saw Liya for the first time, I immediately fell head over heels in love with her. Mrs. Rose wasn't hearing that, and she kept a tight watch on Liya. Liya was popular, so I didn't even know if she would have given me a try anyway. I was so in love with Liya that I wrote a song titled, "Aaliya Bond, I Do Love You." Liya had a younger brother named Tiger, and he and I were pretty cool, and we would always greet each other with a wrestling match that lasted for about fifteen to twenty minutes each time. He always gave me a challenge, which is why I liked when he came around, plus I needed to stay in good with him if I was going to win his sister.

While staying on Hickory, I had reunited with my stepbrother Justin after many years. He lived one street over on Medlock Court, and I had no idea. I begin to hang out with him often. I looked up to him as my big brother; he was cool, handsome, and could play basketball exceptionally well. He would take me to Henderson Gym with him, and I would just watch him play basketball with opponents way older, bigger, and taller than he was. Justin would compete and put them to shame.

He also took me swimming at the Carver Pool and the Boys and Girls Club. Once again he shined. He would come off the diving board and swim faster than I had seen anyone swim. He even had his own set of goggles, which was unusual for a kid during that time.

My reunion with Justin also reunited me with my Grandma Pearl and my Uncle Brave. My Uncle Brave was a Godsend to me and meant the world to me. He would pick Justin and me up, and we would spend the summer doing yardwork, washing cars, and doing other household chores to pay for our school clothing for the year. He set up bank accounts and rewarded us for good deeds and good grades. He also taught us how to play chess and checkers, which played a vital role in my decision-making process.

My Grandma Pearl loved the Lord Jesus, and one of our requirements was to memorize a bible verse every week. We would recite that bible verse during dinner. We always sat down together for dinner as a family. She taught us how to cook, wash clothes, and clean a house. She loved to sing, and she loved to hear us sing. She was big on manners. If you failed to address a grown-up the correct way, you were in deep trouble. She was raising us to be great young men. This time I was not going to lose contact with them, and we stayed in touch.

Like all good things, it had to come to an end. My oldest sister Tabatha and cousin Jose started middle school at South Side Middle School a year before I did. I entered a year after. During that time gangs were on the rise and several groups were forming. I can remember at the beginning of my seventh-grade year a big initiation process for gang members in preparation for the big after-school brawl. I remember one of the recruits being initiated—the other member placed a dog collar around his neck and walked him on all fours around the school building while being paddled.

There were three reasons I could not afford to join a gang. The first reason, I did not approve of people ganging up on someone. Secondly, I did not like fighting, and last, my family would be so disappointed. The family was already going through enough, and I did not need to add to it. Nothing was more important to me than family and not disappointing them.

While all this was going on, we had to move to a new location, out of the two-bedroom apartment into a three-bedroom house on Heard Avenue. The remarkable thing about it was that I had my own room, being the only boy in the house. Lord knows I needed a way out of this school situation, and I needed it fast. My oldest sister and I devised a plan where she would forge my mom's signature to transfer us to another school.

Somehow it worked. The only condition was I had to move in with my Uncle Jared and Aunt Jewel. They were staying with my grandmother temporarily until a place came available. One of the conditions of being transferred to another school was an address requirement to justify going to a specific school. Thank God my Uncle Jared, and Aunt Jewel moved to a location in the district so we could go to the school that was forged on the transfer paper. My sister continued to stay with my grandmother, and I moved in with my uncle and aunt. My sister and I had to meet to catch the bus together. We transferred to Albany Middle School in the middle of my seventh-grade year, and my oldest sister was in the eighth grade. This was tough for many reasons. First reason, it placed a distance between my other two sisters, my cousin Jose, and the girl o f my dreams, Liya. I lost some time.

Transferring to Albany Middle was a time to start fresh and focus on school. The first week of school was testing because I was a new student. At the same time the transfer brought unnecessary attention both good and bad. Even the positive attention turned bad quickly. One thing I knew was that I could not start this new school off with fear and being a coward.

It was only my sister and me. There was no one else, so we had to stick together. My sister seemed to catch on fast to the new changes. She made friends, and things were good for her. For me, on the other hand, things were not so good. I had a run-in with one of the leaders of a gang over a girl whom I did not know or like. So the friends that my sister made assured me that nothing would happen. But they were unable to be around me the entire time. Then I had to fend for myself.

So the hour came near for me and the gang member: "Meet me after school at three o'clock." I could not show any fear, could not run, and had to face it. I knew it was not going to be a one-on-one, and I was certain to get jumped. The plan was to make an example out of just one.

Then something strange happened: a guy by the name of Romeo Drummer intervened on my behalf and said that he knew me and I was "good people." Romeo was not in a gang, but he just knew a lot of people, and apparently his word was enough to get me out of that situation. Romeo and I became instant friends and hung out frequently. Romeo played the drums for the band, for the church, and his mother approved of me. Romeo and I became instant brothers. Romeo also introduced me to my middle school sweetheart. The next year my oldest sister went on to high school while I attended middle school alone. This was the first time I had to attend a school alone, but I had Romeo, so everything was good.

I did not participate in any sports during my time at Albany Middle School. What I did enjoy was my woodworking class. We were able to take wood, sand it down, and add different coats of sealant for protection. I especially liked when we engraved our names in the wood.

I was self-proclaimed "The Love Doctor" because I could put some words down to keep a relationship together or start a relationship. I used to write love letters for my cousins to give to their girlfriends, and at times I would listen in on their conversations and give them words to say to win someone over. I remember bringing a plaque home with Love Doctor on it and showing it to my mom. She looked at me with that "you don't have a clue what love is" look on her face all the while laughing. I got all my lines from songs like "Sweet Love" by Anita Baker, "The Way You Make me Feel" by Michael Jackson, and my favorite "Never Too Much" by Luther Vandross and many more. The look on my mother's face told me the truth—I really was clueless to what love was, but I was in hot pursuit.

3

Rising Waters: The Blood of Protection

Romeo and I completed middle school, but Romeo attended Albany High, and I had to attend Westover High. Somewhere in between all this, my grandmother moved again with my three sisters in an area called Lockett Station Crossing. I remained with my uncle and aunt on Madison.

One of the most tragic natural disasters that happened in Albany, Georgia, was the flood of 1994. This flood struck us at the core and took everything, so I thought. My uncle and aunt moved from Madison to some double-level three-bedroom apartment. All the bedrooms were on the second floor, and the living room and kitchen were located on the first floor. The neighborhood was advised to evacuate the area because the water was rising quickly.

My Aunt Jewel and I were waiting it out until my Uncle Jared got off work. I remember taking a nap and my aunt waking me up telling me we had to go, the water had risen faster than expected. The local authority had to get us to a shallow place by boat so the water would not overtake us. We final reached shallow water, and they let us out.

The water was chest high to me and waist deep to my aunt. She held my hand until we reached the shelter. We waited in a shelter with the rest of the people that evacuated until my uncle arrived.

After that, we all had to move in with my grandmother in her three-bedroom apartment in Lockett Station. My Aunt Diamond and her four kids, my mom with her four kids, and my uncle and aunt and their two kids—all under one roof at one time due to the flood.

Somehow God showed me He did not take everything, but He gave me everything under one roof. One person I have to mention is my cousin Julious. This was the one cousin that loved me and was always excited to see me. The love from family was greatly appreciated, and I loved my cousin and appreciated him for showing me love.

After a couple months, some trailers had come available for those who lost their apartments. My

Aunt Diamond and her family were the first to move out. Shortly after, my Uncle Jared and Aunt Jewel moved out, and of course, I moved with them. I stayed with them until my eleventh-grade year. By that time my mother had fully recovered from her drug addiction, and she got an apartment down the street from her mother and was working at a hospital. I was excited for my mom, so I moved in with her during my eleventh-grade school year. I stayed with her until I moved out at the age of nineteen. Before I tell you how and why I moved out, let me tell you a little bit about my Westover High School years.

Although I attended the same high school for four years, I moved residences four different times. My high school years at Westover High School included being back with my oldest sister, my cousin Jose, and my brother Justin. I truly enjoyed being back with family and having people I knew at school. I also became active in sports and joined the football and wrestling teams. I figured growing up I had enough practice at both. I quickly found out that those outdoor rules of football and the World Wrestling Federation were entirely different from high school rules.

Through those two sports, I met the most amazing coach, Coach Ray Sent. Coach Sent was my football running back coach, my wrestling coach, and my mentor. Not only did he teach me skills on the football field, about wrestling matches, but also life skills. He would check on my grades in the classroom. Coach Sent had stipulations and standards in regard to us playing sports. We had to keep our grades up and maintain a good reputation. I played football to stay in shape for wrestling, and coach inspired me to join the cross country and track teams.

My entire high school years revolved around sports. I was coached into winning the Georgia Regional Championship twice. One year I had to sit out due to a neck injury suffered during a wrestling match. It was kind of disappointing because coach and I had high expectations of winning the state championship that year. At the same time it was kind of funny walking through school with a brace around my neck and students would tap me on the shoulder just to see me turn my whole body and not just my neck.

Coach saw potential in me, potential that I could not see, and perhaps afraid to unleash. He was always in my corner whether I won my match or lost. He would always show me ways I could have improved and never talked down to me. The coach had the ability to see past the noise, my situation, and circumstances and give me sound advice. I am genuinely grateful for Coach Sent.

Playing sports really gave me a genuinely positive outlook on teamwork and brotherly love. I appreciate every teammate that I had the honor to serve with and those from the opposing team that I competed against. I was traveling through the rivers of life, and everyone that I had an encounter with was a part of God's plan for my life. I hear people say that "God works in mysterious ways." On the contrary. God was intentional and deliberate about the purpose, plan, and promise for my life. He was also intentional and deliberate about everyone that I shared moments with.

During this time the river of life was rushing over me and smoothing many rough edges. God was taking me through the world system, which seems to be a consuming fire over my soul and not in a good way. I was in need of something and someone to quench the fire and give rest and peace to my weary soul. It seemed as though I was becoming destructive, wondering, and searching. I was searching for love, chasing the attaboy, accolades, and verbal affirmation in whatever form it came in or which one was the loudest was the direction I ran toward. Love seemed to be temporary and conditional for me. I was trying to find love in sex, in acceptance, money, and places. Still, there was such a void none of those things could fulfill. So the search continued.

One thing that I did not mention was my almost fatal encounter with the Flint River. I mentioned to you the three times I almost drowned and also the flood of 1994. There was another incident where an older gentleman coerced me to go fishing with him at the Flint River. I had never been fishing before, so I was super excited. Without hesitation, we started to dig up earthworms to use for bait and bamboo sticks for fishing poles. He supplied me with the fishing string and hook.

From Mount Zion projects to the Flint River was about a six-mile walk, but we knew shortcuts that reduced time by at least two miles. We finally arrived and got my pole ready, placed my bait on the hook, and I cast it into the water. Suddenly I felt a shove in my back, and I was lunging into the Flint

River. When I looked up for help, I saw the guy laughing and walking away. Two things to this day I cannot remember were how I made it back to the shore, and why did that guy push me in the river.

I was no more than ten years old at the time. I was filled with rage, fear, and shame while walking back alone. I could not tell my mom, because since the water did not kill me she might have and the boy who pushed me. I kept that to myself, and I never went fishing or trusted anyone from that day until later on in life. I am reminded of God's word, "And through the rivers, they will not overflow you." I realized that day that somebody had to be watching over me to have escaped that river.

I mention that I left home at nineteen. Before leaving home, I was in a serious relationship with someone who had a child. I took on the responsibility of parenting before graduating from high school. I did not live up to the things that I promised during that relationship and the father that I set out to be. Seems like I was continuing the path and pattern that was done to me. Men coming in my mother's life promising that they would do something and next day they were gone. Certainly there was no excuse for my actions, but I had to mention that portion of my life, because of the vital role set in the next phase of my life.

After finally graduating from high school I was under this perceived notion that scholarships and job offers were just going to fall in my lap. After all, the only thing that I was told to do was graduate, and everything would fall in place. You had to be pretty naïve to believe that graduating would bring instant success. My only job experience consisted of working in fields pulling plants, and picking pecans, peaches, nectarines, and other plants. We assisted our grandmother to help offset some financial expenses. I worked under the Job Training Partnership Act (JTPA) during the summer of my tenth and eleventh-grade years. One job was at the Boys and Girls Club, and the other was on the Board of Education delivering books and free lunches to different locations. Other than that, I had no real job experience and no plans after graduation.

4

Special Recruit for the Kingdom

If you recall earlier, I mentioned I had an uncle serving in the military. My uncle would come into town to visit the family, and he spent most of that time with his twin brother Jared. This particular time he asked me to come visit him in Lafayette, Indiana. He was scheduled to have oral surgery and would be off work for a while. I had just graduated from high school, no job and nothing back from any colleges, so why not.

I arrived in Lafayette in the summer of 1997, and my uncle went through his surgery and was up and running in no time. He started asking questions concerning my plans in life, my previous grades in school, and my criminal record. First question was easy: I did not have a plan. Second question was easy: good grades. And the third was that when I was a juvenile I was on probation. So he handed me this paper with test questions that had four parts, and he gave me a time limit in which I had to complete it. Kind of confused on where he was going with all this, I took him up on the challenge, and besides this was the only thing that stood in between me listening to my new Boyz II Men record. I did not know the results of that practice test, and I really did not inquire.

The next day I was heading to my uncle's job so he could introduce me to some of his coworkers. After the introduction, he told me he wanted to validate my test results and wanted me to take the real test. This real test unknown to me was an Armed Service Vocational Aptitude Battery Test (ASVAB). One of his employees dropped me off to take the test.

Back at my uncle's apartment, he told me he wanted me to see a doctor to ensure I was still in shape and had no issues from all the sports that I had previously played. Early the next day we headed to Indianapolis, Indiana, in order to make it to a place called Military Entrance Processing Station (MEPS). Now I was thinking how thoughtful it was for my uncle to be concerned about my education and health. There were several other kids there to see the doctor as well.

This MEPS thing seemed like it took me all day, and, finally, my uncle showed up to update me on the results from the doctor. The results were good, so now it was time to head back to the apartment to rest up, so I thought. My uncle asked me if I wanted to talk with the guidance counselor on the results of the test and doctor's exam. Now in my mind, I was thinking guidance counselor like the one at high school, so I agreed. The guidance counselor asked life questions such as what were my passion, interests, and future plans. I was still uncertain at that time, so he pulled up a list of jobs and explained them to me and told me to pick one. I chose a mechanic job. I figured whenever I was able to purchase a car at least I would be able to fix it. It seemed simple enough, a mechanic job, start in September, no-brainer.

Two days later I was heading back to Albany and to let everyone know how my trip went, especially my mom. Now, let's recap: I went to visit my uncle who was a recruiter, did I mention my uncle was an Army recruiter? I took a pre-ASVAB test, took the real test, took a physical, saw a guidance counselor, signed some papers, and headed out in September. Did anybody catch the fact that I just signed up for the Army except me?

My mom was waiting for me to tell her all about my trip. I began to tell her how my uncle, her brother, helped me get a job as a mechanic, and I was to leave for training in September. She gave me a look that pierced me to my core. I cannot remember the last time she gave me a look like that.

In a calm voice she asked if she could see the paperwork. Taking the paperwork, she sat on the couch, and she did something apparently I failed to do, she read. She then explained to me that I had just signed up for three years in the United States Army and was heading to basic training (boot camp) in September at Fort Leonard Wood, Missouri.

My mom had a fit and was so disappointed being that I was her only boy. I felt like an idiot, but God and my uncle must have had a profound conversation concerning my future. Twenty years later this is still the best-unplanned decision I have had the honor of being tricked into. The agreement had been made. The contract had been signed and no turning back.

It did not take long for the family to find out because my mom made sure of that. At the moment, I was having decision remorse. One thing that set me at ease was the joy that it brought my Uncle Jared and Aunt Jewel, whom I spent about two-thirds of my youth with. Their approval was a relief. Now it was time to prepare for basic training and being away from home for an extended period of time. The most I had spent away from home was doing wrestling camp, and that was only for a week. I was faced with a nine-week Basic Combat Training (BCT) and a nine-week Military Occupational Specialties (MOS) training in Fort Leonard Wood, Missouri. Time to step out on my own, become a man, and make a grown-up decision, just as soon as I figured out where Missouri was located.

The time came quickly for me to catch the bus to Florida to swear in for the second time and ship out to basic training. Keep in mind I have not made it out of the rising water and was already heading toward rushing rivers. Although through Christ I am redeemed, I still have not taken the most important step of my life, and that was to give my life over to Christ.

II. God Brought Me Through the World System (The Rivers Plans)

5

Rivers with No Remorse

We arrived in Missouri on the bus, and our initial briefing was pretty decent. The drill sergeant came on the bus to explain to us everything that was going to take place, and life at that moment was good.

We went through reception to get shots, confirmed our contracts, and started our pay. Afterward, we went to the Central Issue Facility (CIF) to get our Table of Allowances 50 (TA 50) and initial issue clothing. Keep in mind I was only 135 pounds. I had my bags that I left Georgia with and now two duffel bags full of gear.

It was time to leave reception and head to the other side of the post where our training would begin. We said our goodbye and thank you to everyone at reception for everything. Thinking to myself I thought that was not so bad, those people were friendly. Surely this is how the remainder of my time will be spent while at basic training. The odd thing about transportation was always being transported in huge groups, for a short distance and everywhere we went. We arrived at the barracks, the cattle truck pulled up (yes, cattle truck), the door opened, and the senior drill sergeant stepped on the bus.

Back at reception, they taught us some customs and curiosity things to get us started. One phrase they taught us was, "AT EASE." When a drill sergeant comes in and out of your area, that is what you yell out and if they are coming in a direction and you need to clear a path you yell, "AT EASE, MAKE WAY." The drill sergeant stepped on the bus, and we yelled, "AT EASE" at the top of our lungs. It was so quiet you could hear a pin drop. He began to welcome us to basic training and give us instruction, and he was not yelling like the movies portrayed. After his briefing, he said he was going to now introduce us to our drill sergeants for the next nine weeks.

He stepped off the bus, and life as we knew it was about to come to a screeching halt. The scene went from good to the inferno. A gang load of drill sergeants came on the bus yelling, screaming, and other choice words. All I heard was "GET OFF THE

BUS," "GET YOUR BAG," "HURRY UP," "NOW," and "MOVE IT." For some reason I could not move, I didn't know if my heart had stopped beating, and all my bodily fluids were doing whatever they wanted to do. I was thinking that it was not real, fake, and just a prank, at least I was praying it was not real. That prayer was short lived. This was real, and I mustered up enough strength to get my bags and get off the bus.

I hobbled off the cattle truck weighted down with my personal bags in one hand, one duffel strapped to the front of my chest and the second duffel bag strapped to my back. It was the end of September, but it felt like the ozone layer had agreed to let the sun come visit the spot we were in for a day. This was not what I signed up for. Why didn't my uncle warn me about this, and would Jesus be able to hear me at this place they call "fort lost in the wood."

Everything inside of me was screaming for help, support, advice, escape, or something to let me know everything was going to be all right. Every day was a struggle for me. I was homesick and confused. I was thinking this was punishment for all the things I had done. The only day the drill sergeant let off on us was Sunday. We used Sundays to call home, but you had to wait in a long line for the pay phone so you had a time limit.

The trick was to memorize your calling card number, every number you needed to call, and hope that they answered. When you did talk to someone, ensuring them to send letters, pictures, and care packages was the number one concern. It was a sad and lonely week if the person you were trying to call did not answer your call or you did not receive a letter. We also did laundry, shined our boots, and did a whole lot of barracks maintenance on Sundays.

I started going to church for some of the wrong reasons, but the word of God seemed to always find its way into my heart. Traveling was never done alone. A battle buddy had to be part of everyone's traveling process. If a solider was caught without a battle buddy, everyone paid the price. So every time I went to church, I had to beg for a battle buddy to go with me. The real reason I went to church was that I found out that the chapel was the only off-limit place that a drill sergeant could not get to you. It was the only place I could find a nap and one of the only places that I was referred to by the name on my uniform.

Ironically the message of God encouraged, motivated, and inspired me to keep going, but on Mondays when the drill sergeants showed up, the word wore off. It did not help that our company symbol was "Hell Hounds." I did not know much about God during that time, but with hound dogs from hell, I knew we were heading in the wrong direction. Only by the Grace of God, the support from my family, and friends, I made it through all three phases of basic training (red, white, and blue) and finally graduation time.

Many of my battle buddies' family members were going to attend their graduation ceremony. I did not even attempt to add that pressure to my family knowing they could not afford to come see me graduate. It was depressing to see them with their families and girlfriends, but I could not let jealousy linger too long.

Most of the soldiers that graduated were going to another duty station for their Advanced Individual Training (AIT), with the exception of three of us. We were just going across the post for school. Our MOS school was located in the same place as our basic training. I could not catch a break. This time we had a little more freedom than before, did not have to ride a cattle truck, and finally got a chance to eat at a fast-food restaurant. After my battle buddies and I finished eating Burger King, we reported to our drill sergeant who was a tad bit approachable, but not much more.

During my basic training time, I experienced a glimpse of God's power working in me, and I knew it was only His power that got me through basic training. However, I was unsure how to activate the power of God. I would get it on Sunday, and as soon as opposition came my way it would wear off. God knew I was not prepared for what was about to come during my next training phase.

6

Psalm 23: Searching for Still Waters

AIT kicked off, and we were well into the Military Occupational Specialty (MOS) in which we would perform at our next duty station. We are also looking forward to going home for Christmas exodus in December.

My MOS was a 62B, which later changed to a 91L (Construction Equipment Repairer)—we worked on land moving equipment like bulldozers, scrapers, graders, rollers, boats, and many more. I really enjoyed that portion of AIT. It was new, and I would officially get to break something without being charged or getting in trouble. I remember being awakened by the Charge of Quarters (CQ) personnel telling me to report to the drill sergeant with a battle buddy. I woke my battle buddy up to come with me to see the drill sergeant.

While walking down the hallway, my battle buddy was asking me what I did wrong, and I was pondering trying to figure the whole thing out. Once I arrived at the drill sergeant's office, I knocked on the door, waited for a reply, and once he answered, I sounded out with, "Drill sergeant PVT Journey reporting to the drill sergeant as ordered."

He told me to enter and have a seat. I knew it was serious because no one ever had a seat in the drill sergeant's office. My heart was beating out of my chest mainly because I was so afraid of drill sergeants. He asked me if I had an uncle by the name of Jared, and I replied with, "Yes drill sergeant."

He told me that my uncle had passed away. The heart that was beating fast was now completely shattered. My battle buddy placed his hand on my shoulder, and I did not know whether to scream, yell, or pass out. The uncle I lost was the twin brother of the uncle that recruited me. He was the closet father figure I had, and never have I personally experienced a loss at that magnitude in my life.

At this point in my life, I did not think it was necessary to continue in the military. I was not taught or equipped to handle such a loss. The drill sergeant showed a soft side that I needed to see during this time and allowed me to make a phone call home. The first person I called was my grandmother Georgia, and when she answered the phone, I said, "Hello, Grandma, is it true that Uncle Jared died?"

There was a pause, and for the first time in my life I heard my grandma weep and reply yes it was true. I could no longer hold the tears back. She began to read Psalm 23 in its entirety. I'd heard this psalm before, but it was different this time. It was as if the words coming from her mouth came through the phone and wrapped its arms around me and brought unexplainable peace. The only reason I embraced joining the Army was to make him proud. My uncle's death gave me an escape route and exit out of the military.

Besides I was homesick. Fort Leonard Wood was no place for me, and those idiots (drill sergeants) with brown hats did not have any Southern hospitality. If you recall I told you that I came into the military weighing 135 pounds. After the death of my uncle, I gained over thirty-seven pounds placing me over the weight limit for my age and height in the military. During that period of my life, I was stressed, depressed, and using food as an outlet. All my uniforms were tight, and they were not issuing me anymore, the sad part about it was that I did not care. God, are you still leading me beside the still waters?

A Story in a Not So Perfect Life

They say a perfect day is when the air is clean and in the daytime the skies are blue;
But what about the days that are hard to explain and my life as a child and all that I've been through.
You see my fantasy as a child was to have the better things in life and never have to worry; So far it's not even close, the bad times are still around and the good times and people are leaving in a hurry. As I compare the two types of people in the world, the rich and the poor;
I'm still finding myself in the same position "neutral" which leaves me no place to go.
You see the poor people always have a smile and full of pride and the rich people are always confused with lots of problems and sorrow; That is why I just count my blessings and live for three days; today, tonight, and tomorrow.
You see I joined the Army not wholly out of choice,
But to make my family happy and let them know I

hear their voices. They say there is a thing as being lucky in life; They say you are lucky when gambling whether playing cards or rolling the dice.
Everything happens for a reason, just like the bad things people go through and the four seasons.
There is much that goes on through my nineteen-year-old mind;
There is a lot I should let go, like my uncle's death.
But it is hard to do, believe me, I have been trying
I try hiding my tears behind my fake smile;
But my silent cries are still heard from miles around.
I think that no one has endured more pain than I have and I know that for a fact;
From a misunderstanding on who's my dad, to a mom that fell victim to crack;
They say only the strong survive and the weak you leave behind;
But who are they to judge when the weak was once strong and for the strong to be strong it took some time.
I cannot say I went through this alone;
Because I have three sisters that are at home who feel their part in life was also written wrong.
I know that all the poems that I wrote are sad and full of drama; but what does the future have in store for me, that is the question I wonder.

I often pollute my mind by telling myself that I am not getting married or planting any seeds; what's leading me to say this, is it my own selfish greed?
All I know is that my life is filled with so many unanswered questions and missions;
Is the answer worth looking for, were my problems worth fixing?
Sometimes reality is the hardest thing to accept and see;
But death is something I can accept because it is the one thing that is promised to me.
My grandmother told me about a perfect God, who have a perfect son called Jesus who paid the price; grandma pray for me that they re-write this story in my not so perfect life.
I can bring joy to a person with just the movement of my pen and
tears of different emotion when the poem ends.

7

Finishing What God Started

I did not attend my uncle's funeral because I was only weeks away from going home for Christmas exodus, and my aunt assured me that my uncle would have wanted me to finish AIT. With the help of the Lord, battle buddies, and family support, I made it to Christmas exodus. I was on leave for fourteen days heading to Georgia.

During my flight I begin to plot going Absent Without Leave (AWOL). My plan was solid; however, there was only one person who could screw this plan up, my grandmother Georgia. Grandmother rescued us from everything else, and this was no different. Two days prior to heading back to AIT, I walked into the garden where my grandmother was. With tears running down my face, nose running, and head down. I said to her, "I am not going back, I am scared, and those men are mean to me."

Grandmother replied, "Look at me, you have to go back and finish up. They will come looking for you."

Grandma put down her garden tool and picked up her bible. She gave me this promise that changed my mind completely when she read from Deuteronomy 31:6: "Be strong and courageous. Do not be afraid or terrified because of them, for the Lord your God goes with; he will never leave you nor forsake you." After hearing those words coming from her mouth, from that book, I was ready to go find my purpose and fulfill it. I returned to Leonard Wood and my contract and commitment.

I made it through the initial phase of the Army, received my follow-on assignments, and they were sending me to Fort Irwin, California, one of the farthest places from Georgia. I was going from Missouri, a state where I experienced snow for the first time to where all four seasons happen in one day in the Mojave Desert. At this time I was thinking I should have taken the AWOL gig that I was planning and disregarded my grandmother's advice.

After saying farewell to my battle buddies—some I was hoping to never see again and some I wanted to keep in touch with, but I knew I was not going to make an effort. I thought they were going to place me on a long bus ride; instead, they issued me a flight ticket. I'd never flown in a plane before, but I was about to get a small glimpse of heaven. I was going to experience a lot of firsts and lasts during my tour in California.

Nightfall had set in when I arrived, which made it hard to get a view of our environment. Once we arrived at reception, they gave us instructions and told us to bed down and report the next day for more instructions. When we woke up the next day, and I walked outside, I was met by a dry heat, sand, and coyotes.

Matthew 4:1 starts off saying, "Then Jesus was led by the Spirit into the wilderness to be tempted by the devil." The only thing that I had to do with the previous sentence was change Jesus' name to Johnny. Where am I, Lord, and why? During my Fort Irwin experience, I did many first-time things. I was ignorant to the value of money and how to manage it. My lack of understanding the value of money led me to living check to check, and when I did get the next check, my account already reflected a negative balance. This was my first time having two jobs and still experiencing days of being broke and hungry, not to mention I had no one to blame but myself.

I got my first and only tattoo by way of peer pressure. This was my first time getting drunk to the point of alcohol poison, and my last time ever drinking again. My first time I accepted Jesus as my Lord and Savior without being mandated. Although it was not quite personal yet, I took the first step. I attended church regularly on my own and not under compulsion of the stress of drill sergeants. I went through the resume, interview, and hiring process on my own for the first time. This was the first time the realization of every decision I made from this point on would reflect what type of man that I currently was and would become.

One of the most difficult decisions that I had to accept was that I had no more excuses and could not blame anyone for my failures and shortcomings. I would spend the next three years of my life in California at the National Training Center (NTC), where I made rank quickly from Private to Sergeant in two years. I bought my first car in California. In California you go through all the preliminaries of buying a vehicle, they allow you to drive the car home, and later they tell you that you did not get approved for the car loan. At least that's what happened to me, so I had to shamefully drive the car back three hours from where I picked it up.

Although I worked all the time, I always found time for sports. I played on the company flag football team where we won post championship twice, and I started back wrestling. The goal was to wrestle for the post and build my stats to compete for the All-Army wrestling team. I trained in folkstyle wrestling, but to compete in a tournament I had to know freestyle and Greco-Roman style. I had two coaches in California who specialized in freestyle and gymnastics and the other in Greco-Roman.

My unit allowed me to participate in wrestling practice during Physical Training hour (PT). It helped that I maxed my PT test with a 300 after getting all that stress weight off my body. Now that was a good news story from a kid who failed his first PT test in the Army, was overweight due to overeating caused by stress, and now this physically fit soldier was fueled by a passion for getting better.

We traveled around California and Georgia to participate in a tournament to build my stats so that I could apply for All-Army. The only thing

I was missing was the passion, and without the desire, this wrestling journey quickly came to an end and placed my focus on my military career. It just was not the same being in the military, working at the movie theater, and not having a Coach Sent. From that season on, I pursued hard after my military career, learning my craft as a mechanic and focusing on building a relationship with Christ.

8

God Taught Me How to Hold a Tune

I have not so far mentioned my previous relationships and past girlfriends. I would be remiss if I didn't tell you a love story that baffled even me to this day. By no means am I disregarding or belittling any of my previous relationships, I truly treasured those moments, and I learned from them.

One of the most exciting times I looked forward to was going on leave (vacation). I would save six months of leave, that's two and half days a month, which totaled fifteen days. I was a week out from going on vacation and my roommate at the time was listening to a song by an artist name Jewel. Most single soldiers stayed in the barracks with a roommate of the same gender, similar to college dorms. At that time, I listened to a lot of hip hop, rhythm and blues, and oldies but goldies. My roommate listened to mix music mostly pop, heavy metal, and hip hop. On this particular day, he was listening to this song that caught my ear, and I asked him about the album. We sat down and listened to each song. He explained them all and let me borrow his compact disc (CD). The song is essential in the love story so keep this in mind.

Do you recall Aaliya Bond who stayed on Hickory Lane, next door to Aunt Diamond, whose grandmother would not take her eyes off her, whose brother I wrestled with, and the Liya I wrote the song for? Yes, that Aaliya. Well while in California, I heard from a valid source that Liya's mom moved next door to my grandmother. I had not seen or heard from her in almost ten years. I am sure a lot had taken place between those years.

The day finally arrived when I could go on leave. I was always welcome with open arms from my family, and the feeling was still mutual. Upon arriving I spent time with family and friends, but I was also trying to figure out how to bring myself to verify if Tasha's mom lived next door and if so how could I get in touch with Liya.

This particular day I was leaving my mom's house walking toward my grandma's house, and from a distance, I see this female, I knew she was not from the neighborhood. I did not catch a glimpse of the apartment she entered. At the same time, one of my relatives had just made a cat call toward the girl getting out of the car. So I asked him, "Who was that girl?" and I cannot recall if he gave me an answer or not. I went to my grandmother's house and chatted with her for a while. I made a phone call to my source to get the exact location of Liya's mother's apartment.

It just so happened the girl who stepped out of the car was Liya! She was at her mom's house at that time. I went to the apartment, knocked on the door, and her mom answered and greeted me with a friendly hug. She called Liya to the door as I waited on the outside. She did not tell Liya who awaited her at the front door. It seemed like forever before she arrived at the door or I just could not wait. She finally came, and I was speechless when I saw her.

She was beautiful and stunning. We chatted briefly and made plans for later on that day. We conversed over the phone, and the next day she picked me up, and we went to the mall and over to my oldest sister's house. My oldest sister was cooking while we were over and needed something from the grocery store. Liya and I volunteered to walk to the store to get the item. While we were walking, Liya started softly singing a song, and I chimed in and finished it. The song she was singing was from the artist Jewel, the one my roommate played back in California and introduced to me.

She looked at me in total amazement, and I understood why. It was uncommon for African American males during that time to know and listen to Jewel, let alone sing the song. That was the spark that lit the fire, who would ever have guessed a song would bond us together. Liya was saved, had a job, and was attending college. She made it clear that she had a daughter, was not looking for a boyfriend, and the next relationship would be her future husband. That was a taboo word for me. I was unsure I would be able to measure up to being a dad, let alone a husband.

I went back to California with much to think about and still a lot to learn. Liya and I often talked while I was in California, and she was now part of my day. I did not want to lose her again but still had not committed to the husband commitment. We booked her first flight to visit me in California, where we vacationed at SeaWorld and hung out with friends and church members.

The trip went well, and by this time I was head over heels for her. She returned to Albany, and I finished up my tour in California. Since my military career was going well, I decided to reenlist for three more years. I was able to pick Fort Benning, Georgia, as my duty station of choice. Albany was about an hour from Fort Benning, which gave me the opportunity to spend more time with family and build on the relationship that Liya and I had started. Little did I know I was about to answer a call that was going to reshape my entire existence on earth. I bid farewell to my friends, whom I still keep in contact with, notably Chris Tweet and Tim Brother.

It was time to make some decisions now since I was moving back to Georgia on a Permanent Change of Station (PCS) to Fort Benning. It was the year 2000, and we survived the Y2K end of the world, and I was twenty-two.

First, I had to decide on the institution and permanency of marriage and all that comes with marriage. This decision is baffling, because marriage is an institution that is of God and I was clueless to what

God says about marriage. Other competing factors clouded my judgment. One thing that I was not uncertain about was whether I was in love. Second, I had to get a car, and I don't want to report to a new duty station with no vehicle. I wanted to be able to come home for the weekend to secure my favor from God and Liya. One thing I did know at that time was Proverb 18:22: "He who finds a wife finds a good thing and obtains favor from the LORD." During that time, I did not have a revelation of the scripture, but I knew it applied to me. I knew I had found a good thing, and to obtain favor was yet to come.

"Through God, financial hardship is a thing of the past for our family. It was over nine years ago that financial hardship hit our family after a downfall in the real estate market, which generated a large sum of our family income. During this season of our life, we carried over $130,000 in debt, not including our homes. During this hardship, our income decreased to a one family income, and we had to sell our home, turn a vehicle back into the dealership, and lost rental property. We learned many lessons during that season of our life, however, through it all, we

have been restored, our finances have been restored, and a life of debt freedom is in our view within the next year. We serve a faithful God."

— Mike and Sylvia McClean

9

Favor from the Savior

Now it was time to look for a car, which was turning out to be one of the biggest disappointments of my life. This was a time where I found out the importance of credit, and my credit was bad.

I had no clue how bad my credit was, nor how all the bad accounts got attached to my credit report. Again I was in the process of trying to buy a car, and the devastating part was I had no one who would co-sign for me. On top of that, every dealership that I was going to was pulling my credit report and making a lousy report worse.

Liya and I went through my credit report, paid off all past due accounts, and closed out things that were zero balance. We also requested a letter stating the account had been paid in full and closed out. Some unpaid debt went to the credit bureau; some were paid off as we called to negotiate with the creditors. I was about a week out from signing off leave and still no car.

Finally, I found the car that I was determined to get. I went back to the bank. The clerk ran my credit and told me that I had weak credit and was unable to help me. I walked away frustrated and upset, but just before I walked out of the bank, something rose up in me and told me not to give up so quickly. I turned around, and I explained to the clerk that I was in the military, I had no kids, I just paid off all my debt, I had no one to co-sign for me, and I got paid once a month. I assured her with tears rolling down my face if she gave me a chance to prove myself, I would not disappoint her and would not miss a payment.

She looked at me, got up out of her seat, and said, "Give me a moment." She walked into another office and shut the door. I was still standing in the place where I made my plea and ten minutes passed before the lady came back in the room.

She said, "I don't know what it is about you, but I believe you and the bank is going to give you a chance." She also explained that my interest would be high. I did not care. I needed a car, did not have a co-signer, and more importantly needed a favor.

I left the bank approved for my first car—a 1997 Mazda Millenia. I paid that car off years later and went back looking for that lady to thank her for taking a chance on me. Now I understood the "obtain favor from the Lord." I could finally start my new job with a good impression and get back and forth to home and work.

Meanwhile, Liya was planning the wedding of the century, and she had already planned the date: August 25, 2001. She paid for rings and worked on the guest list. Things were happening so fast that the traditional get down on one knee, ask the father can I marry your daughter and having the money was out the window for me. I wanted to propose to her on one knee, and I wanted to ask her dad if I could marry her, but I let doubt and fear keep me from giving her what she deserved.

Things were going well on the job. I was in the 608th Ammunition Company, working as a shop foreman. My responsibility was to keep the equipment running and be able to brief the status of the equipment and personnel. I was always able to work well with others, make new friends, and follow direction from those appointed over me.

I would leave on Friday afternoon to travel home to Albany and would not come back to my barracks room at Fort Benning until 0300 Monday mornings. I would attend church some Sundays with Liya. When I did visit, the word was right on time, but I knew at the end of service I had to answer the Deacons of the church about my intentions with Liya. I thought they were haters, but they were able to see that not all my attentions were godly and they had her best care in mind.

Looking back on them I'm glad they did. It kept me on a straight and narrow path. Months passed and it was getting close to the wedding, all the planning was done. We had a couple more things to pay off, and we were ready to move forward. I was getting super nerves, anxious, and hoping I don't mess anything up. I was scheduled to have two best men and eight groomsmen. Liya was expected to have one maid of honor, one matron of honor, and eight bridesmaids. The guest list had well over 200 in attendance. It was hard for me to believe an event like this was going to take place. Besides, the only time gatherings of this magnitude took place was at a funeral.

The big day was upon us. August 25, 2001, had arrived and it was super crazy that day, getting everyone together, making sure that we kept unity, and my only responsibility was to bring the rings. Speaking of rings, two weeks before the wedding I decided to play basketball and jammed my ring finger on the left hand. We had to reorder my wedding ring. A couple weeks after the wedding, my ring finger went back to normal, and we had to add a guard to the ring.

The marriage was delayed for about thirty minutes because I forgot the wedding rings. The rings arrived, and the wedding was on its way. The entire wedding was something that you would view on television. We pulled it off! We planned a year for the wedding, and Lord knows more thoughts should have been placed on preparing the marriage. After the wedding, we rode to our reception with the limousine gift that my cousin Warren had bought for us. Family and friends sang the lyrics I wrote for her back on Hickory, the street where I first meet her, and we danced the night away.

It was merely God who could have arranged all of that and placed us together. I am now the husband to Aaliya, a father to Shadona (Dona), and the man of the house. I moved the family to Fort Benning. We begin our life as a family together.

10

Your Identity and Truth Are in the Blood

My first two weeks of marriage was spent out in the field during a Field Training Exercise (FTX). Then the unspeakable happened: the 9/11 terrorist attack.

We had to pack up and leave the area and man the gates until things got sorted out. I could not go off post for a week due to traffic. When it was finally time for me to leave the job to travel back home, a soldier leaving guard duty rear ended me in my vehicle. No matter how long or short I was gone due to the military commitment, Liya and Dona would always receive me with open arms and were sincerely happy to see me. I did not know how to accept that kind of love. It was almost too good to be true.

One of the biggest mistakes that I made when I got the title "married" pinned on me. I took that word out of content and put undue stress, pressure on myself, and lost track of our friendship that we had before marriage. It was time to find a church home for the family. I knew at this rate something so good could turn bad quickly without proper spiritual guidance.

There were still so many questions in my life that needed answers and closure. If you recall earlier in the book, I mention I used to ask my mom why my dad did not come see me. My grandma on my paternal side used to always ask me, "Have your mom told you the truth about your dad?" I never could understand that question, and besides my name was Johnny Lee Journey Jr., and my mom used to be married to Johnny Lee Journey Sr. at some point, and he was paying child support. I could not figure out for the life of my youthful mind why that question was constantly being brought up. I used to always go back and tell my mom, and she assured me that Johnny Lee Journey Sr. was my daddy, he was a good man and don't worry about any of that.

I can remember when I was younger, there were several attempts made to take a blood test, but each attempt was unsuccessful. More than anything I wanted to know the truth and wanted the truth to be that Johnny Sr. was my father. Before departing California, I reached out to him for advice concerning marriage, and he gave me sound advice from his military experience. He also corrected me on placing a lower-case "g" on God. I told him all about Liya and where she worked, what she did and how I was head over heels about her.

Johnny Sr. even went to visit Liya on her job while I was in California. Liya began to boast about how he came to visit her, and it helped seal my relationship with her. He even talked about how he had been tracking my career from high school sports and the military. So I decided at the age of twenty-two to ask him permission to take a blood test, and I would pay for it.

He agreed, and we met up and took the blood test. Afterward, Liya, Johnny Sr., and I stood outside the blood test facility chatting. I can remember just hoping and wishing the test results would prove that he was my father. About two weeks later I was on my way from Fort Benning back to Albany when I received a phone call from Liya stating that the test results had arrived. I asked her not to open it until I get to her apartment. My heart and mind were going a hundred miles an hour with doubt, fear, and what-ifs. Finally, I arrived at the residence, she handed me the letter, and I paced around with it for a moment. I took a seat on the couch, Liya gave me the room for a moment.

I conjured up enough nerves to open the letter, and it was like a scene from the TV show *Maury* as the audience was awaiting the test results only this time there were no commercial breaks. The test results were in and Johnny Lee Journey Sr. was NOT the father. The feeling I had when my Uncle Jared passed was the same feeling that came upon me, but the pain was ten times worse. I was not alone, Liya was that battle buddy this time. This would be the first time that Liya saw me break down and cry as a man. I wanted to restrain myself, but I could not. I truly wanted Johnny to be my dad, and I did not want my mom to be wrong. I was also concerned about my relationship with my Uncle Brave and my brother Jermaine. We had built such a strong bond, I could not stand the sight of losing them.

I was and still am to this day protective of my mother and her feelings. The last thing I wanted to do was to have my mom put to shame. It took me a while to recover that day. I knew I had to tell my mom and have this conversation with Johnny Sr. about the results. I must say that I was angry and lashed out at people who were close to me. That is when I learned that I would never again say things that I would have to apologize for later. My mom and I had a heartfelt talk after I cooled down, as she shared with me the reasoning behind what she thought happened. She was sure that he was my dad all the way up to when I showed her the results. She did not play the blame game nor did she throw a pity party. She ended the conversation stating that Johnny was a good man and that as my mom she did not mean to hurt me and she loved me.

I believe it was a relief for both of us that truth was brought into the light. A good friend and pastor who I will talk about later in this book used to say, "It is not the truth that will set you free, but the truth that you know that will set you free." I was free from that but not free indeed, and still, the question remains who is my father?

Not long after this heartbreaking finding, I was introduced to my father, Ben Sikes and my four new sibling Lora, Luke, Lucy, and Luna. Over the last thirteen years, we have built a relationship with my new inheritance family. I must say they are a phenomenal family that welcomed me with open arms. I spent most of those moments with the late Angel Sikes. I know she found her resting place in heaven with God. No matter how things were going in her life, good or bad, she would always say, "Do not worry about me, because God got me."

God certainly had her in the palm of His hands and her entire family. Now I have four more beautiful siblings to love on and a heaven load of aunts, uncles, nephews, nieces, cousins, and friends. My dad and I are steadily building on our relationship with each other and with Christ. Special thanks to Aunt Kindle Eve for keeping it together and ensuring the family received me into the family fold.

"From the time we accepted Jesus Christ as our personal Savior and made a conscious decision to serve Him, we have come to realize that God is the ultimate source of our peace, strength, and joy. Through the many fiery trials, oppositions, setbacks, frustrations, and disappointments, it is by the Grace of God that has brought us through every situation. It is through His strength that always gave us the ability to rise back up through the toughest of times. We truly understand that we must always have faith in

God and with God on our side, we always win. It is through the power of God that we have been able to withstand, knowing that no weapon formed against us will prosper. We have held on to Isaiah 43:2 as a prophetic word for our lives:

"When you pass through the waters, I will be with you; And through the rivers, they will not overwhelm you. When you walk through fire, you will not be scorched, Nor will the flame burn you."

— (Isaiah 43:2 Ampl) To God be the Glory

— James and Pam Williams

11

Rivers of Rejection through God

I knew if I wanted to succeed in my marriage, as a father and husband, I had to find a church home and fast. Some refer to the first years of marriage as the toughest, and if you endured the first year, you were going to be on the right path.

I remember going to work one day, and a coworker asked me if my wife and I had a church home. She invited us to visit her church. The name of the church was Interdenominational of Faith. The pastors were James and Pamela Williams. I talked to my wife about it, and she agreed that we would visit. We arrived and were bombarded with hugs, welcomes, and handshakes.

Liya was accustomed to that type of hospitality. She attended church frequently and apparently that was the universal church language. Now I was wondering whether this was for real, because there is no way that someone could love a stranger, hug a stranger, and sincerely mean it. It was similar to how Liya and Dona greeted me when I came home from work. For some reason, I rejected that kind of love and affection and could not figure out why maybe I did not want to experience any rejection.

That particular Sunday Pastor James was preaching on the subject of relationships, and he shared a testimony of his first years of marriage. He was very transparent and seemed as though he had a personal conversation with God about me coming to the church with my problems. He also cleared up this myth that I had about pastors being perfect, did not make a mistake, and never had any issues.

Later the church name was changed to Love and Restoration. The theme of the church was Restored for God's Glory. It was godly timing that I had found a church home for the family. I was attempting to position myself as the head of the house by more than just lip service. My family and I became very active in the church. We had great godly men and women as a positive, godly example to look toward.

My first service in the church was the clean-up committee and media. In the church, Minister Deric Overton coached and mentored me through all of the training. He was active duty military as well and also gave me professional development. Most of the time I would home in on the pastor, his teachings, and his compassion for the people. I was still dealing with some personal issues such as music, idolizing material things, and coveting. God surrounded me with men who were not ashamed and admitted they were delivered with some of the same issues. They also provided me with ways to deal with issues.

For example, I loved listening to music, all kinds of music. The closer I drew to God, the more the type of music I was listening to could not fill the void. I was trying to figure out why the worldly music was not having the same effect it used to have over me. I was introduced to various Gospel artists and Christian rap artists to replace the other artists I was accustomed to hearing. I realized how vital the scripture in Matthew 16:19 (King James Version) "And I will give unto thee the keys of the kingdom of heaven: and whatsoever thou shalt bind on earth shall be bound in heaven: and whatsoever thou shalt loose on earth shall be loosed in heaven."

A simple way I understood it then was if I bind music up or music that doesn't bring glory to God in my life, then someone or myself had to lose some music that does bring glory to God in my life.
That is what was happening around me during that time. God was positioning me for His glory. Still, I had not committed to Him yet. My entire family recommitted our lives over to Christ and got baptized at Love and Restoration Church, and things were moving in a proper direction. By this time, I was going on two years at Fort Benning and a little over a year in my marriage and about the same time in the new church.

Meanwhile, on my job, we were still getting accustomed to functioning after the 9/11 terrorist attack, and my unit received orders to deploy. We underwent some extensive training and certification in preparation for deployment. The unit deployment would be an effort push for more soldiers to relieve others that were already deployed. We were to take the majority of our home station equipment. It was at the same time the Army selected me to attend recruiting school.

During that time the Army used to send Personnel Command (PERSCOM) messages in the mail to notify a soldier of his or her duty assignment. In my little over five years' experience in the Army, I was thinking deployment took precedent over recruiting. I never mentioned much about recruiting although somebody in the unit had to be tracking this particular area. Besides, I wanted to deploy with the team. I was not going to tell my mom, because I knew she was going to pull the only-son card and perhaps jeopardize my career. I did not want to tell my wife, because I knew she certainly would not understand the reasoning behind my wanting to deploy.

About a month out from reporting to recruiting school and about four months out from deployment, I was summoned to the Command Sergeant Major (CSM) office. I knew this was not good at all—a SGT/E-5 directed to report to CSM/E-9. When I arrived, he asked me, "Did you know you were on orders for recruiting?"

I just got into this church thing so I did not think this would be a good time to lie. So I answered with a yes, and he asked me if I told anyone else in my chain of command. I answered no. He directed me to cease all activity toward deployment, get all the necessary paperwork together to go to school, and put in my leave form as well. He also charged my

Section Sergeant and Platoon Sergeant with ensuring this happened.

I felt like a complete failure and coward that I could not deploy with the team that I had worked so hard to get prepared. The worse part was telling soldiers in my squad my recruiting assignment took precedent over the war. Then I had to try to explain to my wife what was going on, which was quite difficult because I was so behind on getting prepared for school, I did not know where to start. Another person I had to explain what was going on was my pastor. He fought tooth and nail to try to get me at least a recruiting station in Columbus, Georgia. He called and wrote letters to proxy for me. I believed Pastor James would have called everyone except the president. I was in such awe that someone of his stature would think so much of me to go through so much trouble. I finally had a glimpse of unconditional love. Even while I was in recruiting school, he was calling, praying, and advising me on what steps to take.

While I was at recruiting school, one of the requirements was to have interpersonal skills, and one of my instructors went around asking us to display our interpersonal skills in any form. He made his way around to me. I could only think of one song to sing, and that song was called, "Ain't No Sunshine" written by Bill Withers. Afterward, my instructor took me to every department to sing that song. One office he took me by was the assignment department where he had me sing the song to them. I had to have sung that song at least eight times that day. During that same time, they were asking us for a list of places that we would like to recruit. Although it was not a guarantee, they would do their best. After singing to the assignment section, I requested that I get Columbus, Georgia, as my recruiting station of choice. She came back a week later and told me she was able to get me the assignment that I requested, Columbia, South Carolina.

That was a total mix-up in Columbus and Columbia, besides the spelling. One was in Georgia; the other was in South Carolina. It was also too late to change it, and everything was locked in. I told my pastor about the mix-up, and he gave godly clarity to the situation. I was beginning to think I got selected for recruiting by way of my uncle who enlisted me.

After recruiting school I headed back to Georgia to prepare the family for our move to South Carolina. One of my proudest moments on some personal note while at Fort Benning was the completion of my associate degree in business from Troy State University. One of the most challenging and trying times was being denied promotion to Staff Sergeant. The sad part about being rejected was the fact it was not due to being ill-prepared nor poor performance. It was due to the president of the board saying I was too young and had not been through enough to be recommended.

This was the first time I spoke up for myself. I asked how about my performance and my knowledge about the question on the board and the CSM agreed. He still insisted that I was too young and did not recommend me for promotion although all the rest of the board members maxed me out on the board. A lengthy discussion took place after I left. I could not understand what I needed to do to get better if I had no recommended improvements. My wife was at home waiting for the results of the board, because she spent countless hours helping me prepare.

When I walked through the front door, she knew the results from the look on my face. It did not go well. I remember telling her that day, I was getting out of the Army frustrated, confused, and feeling defeated. She comforted me and told me to give the pastor a call. After cooling down, I reached out to the pastor to explain what happened on the board. I was not recommended because I was too young, lacked experience, and had not been through enough. The pastor prayed with me, told me this was only a test and that my setback was a setup for something more significant. I did not understand everything, but it was enough to bring me to my senses and able to face tomorrow.

The next day one of the board members told me that she filed a complaint on my behalf, because the president of a promotion board was not a voting member, he was just there to ensure the board ran fairly. She also stated I would be going to another board at another battalion the following week. The information she gave me was confirmation that God had angels camped all around me, and although weapons formed, they could not prosper. I told my wife and pastor the good news.

The following week I went to the board and blew it out of the water. After the board I remember thanking God and asking Him why he was doing all this for me. If only I understood then what I know about God's love and His glory, that would have never been a question. It wasn't now and will never be about me, but all about His love, glory, church, people, and kingdom. It was apparently based on my action in the next chapter that I still did not have a full understanding of God the Father, God the Son, and God the Holy Spirit.

"Through God is why my wife and I are together after thirty-one years and married for twenty-seven. We have seen some rough times. However, we have been able to weather the storms, good and bad. Some of the storms came to try our faith and were orchestrated by God to get us back on the right track. Other storms were self-inflicted storms where we allowed the enemy to come into our marriage and run rampant. My wife and I gave our lives over to Christ, and that is when we began to understand what marriage was all about indeed. Being told that we were too young and our marriage wasn't going to last automatically placed us at bat with two strikes against us. It was in 1994 with three years of marriage and four years in the military that my wife became fed up with our relationship. She was done, wanted out, and she left. God spoke to me, through the television concerning my marriage and marital problems. I made a vow to God if He would fix my marriage that I would serve Him and Him alone. After repeating the prayer of faith and accepting

Christ as my Lord and Savior, immediately the presence of God invaded the room. After over three months of her being gone, a disappointing thirteen-hour trip from Georgia to Indiana to pick her up and instead to hear her say she wasn't coming back, and now the enemy placing thoughts of doubt in my head; my wife finally called saying she was ready to come home. God wants to turn your life around so that others who may be going through some of the same storms you're experiencing will know that nothing is impossible 'Through God.'"

— Deric and Rebecca Overton

III. Broke Through My Hurt, Habit, and Hang-ups (The Fires of Promise)

12

Choose This Day Friend or Foe

Out of the water into the fire, the fire of no longer being a young adult but a man, facing major decisions. This PCS would be the first time my family and I PCS'd together. This posed a challenge for me, because I was accustomed to traveling alone.

We moved out of our apartment, said our sad goodbyes to our military friends, church family, and loaded up heading to Columbia, South Carolina. The movers had already picked up our household goods, and everything was moving in the right direction. My wife and I had a plan to drop our daughter off at her mom's house. Our daughter would stay with my mother-in-law until we got settled in South Carolina.

Since my orders had Columbia Recruiting Battalion, I assumed that Columbia area would be an excellent place to look for an apartment. I was unaware that the battalion had several recruiting stations that covered cities across the state of South Carolina. At the time I took thirty days leave, we spent about a week and a half in my in-laws' home. It was at that time I decided to reach out to an old girlfriend through email to share my thoughts on how I felt my marriage was going. It did not matter the intent nor the content of the email. I could not blame the devil. I certainly could not blame my wife and child. I was entirely out of line, and that act was unacceptable. I sent the email out two weeks prior to my wife finding out.

This is how things progressed during that time. My wife and I arrived in South Carolina in search of an apartment on our own, which was quite challenging to do when you are unfamiliar with an area. She and I walked into a real estate office and inquired about apartments. The realtors look at us kind of funny. It was more like judging us for being too young and not knowledgeable about real estate.

After a while, they assigned us to an agent. The agent asked us if we had ever considered buying a home. Buying a home never crossed our minds. Our mind-set was apartments while growing up, buying a house was at least from my side for the rich. He explained the benefits, simplified things, and asked if he could run our credit.

Now at this point, I knew we were not going to qualify for a house, which was merely the poverty mind-set that I had. When I looked over at my wife, she had that look to say it is up to me on this decision and I took a leap. We were approved for $110, 000 combined, which was suitable for a starter home in that area. He drove us around to view several houses in different areas. After about three days of searching for a home we finally found a home, and we were super excited. We felt as if we had met a milestone in our lives and God was working everything out on our behalf. Due to the closing date, we could not move in until later; therefore, we continued to stay at the Extended Stay Hotel.

During that time, I started in-processing to the battalion, turned in paperwork, and attended a mandatory new recruiter course at the battalion. My wife stayed back at the hotel because she too was getting familiar with the area and looking for a job. One day after in-processing I came in from work to the room and Liya was crying. I did not have to ask why, because I was greeted with the email that I had sent to an ex-girlfriend. I could not lie, I was embarrassed, ashamed, and knew I hurt her and let her down. I did not feel all those emotions because I got caught. I felt terrible because I never wanted to see my wife hurt. She was hurt, and it was my fault. One would have thought that I cheated or something, but it was the principle of trust that had been broken.

At that moment in time, I explained to my wife what was going through my mind during the time I wrote the email. She said she needed time to think about some things. She stayed in the bedroom area of the hotel room. I went to the living room area. Although I had apologized to my wife and I was unsure whether or not she received my apology, my heart was heavy. I could not shake it this time. I could not run this time, and I could not deny it.

I broke down that day and cried out to Jesus. I confessed to Him that very day in the hotel. Lord, I understand that I messed up and it is all my fault. If my wife and daughter leave me because of this email, they have every right. I do not deserve them, and they certainly do not deserve to be treated this way. Lord, when and if I wake up in the morning and my wife is gone, I truly understand, all I'm asking is that you do not leave. I promise if you do not leave me, I will serve you with all I have for the rest of my life. I tried to stay up waiting for an answer.

That morning I woke up and my wife was still there, we talked about the situation. I told her the promise that I made to God and how her even being there is His way of answering. I needed that real repentance in my life, at that time and in that season. By no means was I boasting, bragging, or proud of the way things happened. If I could pick a biblical apostle to help me describe what I went through, it would undoubtedly be Paul and his Damascus Road experience in Acts chapter nine. Whenever I did something that brought discredit to God and his kingdom, I was persecuting God.

Finally, God stopped me through my wife, shined some light on the situation (email), and popped the question about why are you persecuting me. I cannot express how that day was my altar call, where I gave my life over to Christ, and made him my personal Lord and Savior. The father I always wanted was now present in my life, because I let Him in after waiting for so long. He also assured me that He had never left me nor forsaken me and was going to be with me all the days of my life. I chose my side, and that was the side of the Lord.

The next thing on the agenda was to find a church home, a covering, and a place to worship. We found out during that moment that being covered in prayer, by the right people, was necessary for accountability purposes and to ward off any attacks that the enemy may try to plot on our family. It was amazing to witness the power that repentance, God's forgiveness, and forgiving others have a positive outcome. My wife could have gotten on the phone and told her family, my family, and the pastor what had happened in our marriage. Instead, she covered me in prayer, kept me in my position as the head of the house, and allowed me to build trust back in our relationship.

13

Through the Fire: Don't Stop, Drop, or Roll

We headed back to my mother-in-law's house to pick up our daughter and moved into our new home. It was close to school to start for our daughter. We wanted to ensure she was part of the moving process. Liya started her job at a hospital and had an early morning shift. I completed the new recruiter program and was assigned to Sumpter Recruiting Station, which was a forty-minute drive from the house every day. I was charged with ensuring that our daughter was put on the bus every morning. Let us just say the way I did her hair in the morning was not always the way she returned from school, but I did my best.

At this point in my career, I was a six-year in-service promotable sergeant. I reported to the recruiting station with three other brand-new recruiters. The recruiting station was short personnel and had four brand-new, fresh out of recruiting school soldiers in one location. That would prove to be too much for one station commander.

Let me just tell you up front that recruiting duty was the toughest assignment I have ever had even until this day. Recruiting duty taught me how to deal with the views of the public. How to relate to different age groups, genders, backgrounds, races, ethnicity, and rejection. We had to study the regulations, know and ask for an interpretation of the regulations at all times. It was during the peak of the war where the foxholes had to be filled and fast. The word mission was never more apparent than in recruiting. The station commander and other experienced recruiters had a drive and a hunger for mission success like I had never seen before. I wanted that drive. I guess I wanted it in a glass bottle or magic potion to drink. Maybe they could download it into the hard drive of my heart, and I would get it.

Eight months into recruiting I finally got promoted, and my cutoff had dropped from 798 to 791. That new rank came with more expectations, responsibilities, and demands. I struggled for my first two years in recruiting duty, but I never threw in the towel.

There were always teammates and leaders pouring into my life. They saw more in me than what I saw in myself based on the results. Finally, after two years the station started to work together as a team and stopped working as individuals. That drive, passion, and zeal for the accomplishment of the mission was no longer adventitious, but inherent nature. The four of us finished recruiting successfully, and we left the recruiting command with our Gold Badge and Recruiter Ring of Excellence. I also received my first look for Sergeant First Class, but I knew I was not ready. I did not even know how to update my records.

Some may ask what kept me stable or how I didn't lose my mind, and why didn't I throw in the towel? One of the warnings while in recruiting school was if you had a stable marriage, it would survive recruiting duty. If you came in with a rocky marriage, you would leave rocky or divorced. I knew that it was important that we bounce back quickly from my poor choice and that I found a church home for my family. Just so happened that one of my wife's coworker's father's was a pastor. He pastored in a church called New Life Fellowship, and she invited Liya out to visit the church. We attended the church several times before committing to join. Once we committed to join, we reached out to our previous pastor in Georgia and told him about the plan to join the church. He and some other members of the church drove from Georgia to South Carolina, conducted a church service at the Holiday Inn, and transferred us over to New Life Fellowship.

"Through God, our life is the Lord's project, and we have surrendered our agenda to his will. When we turn things over to him and humbly submit to his directions, then we find that our life is right on schedule, and find that we are in his good and perfect will. God sent us to the people we minister to on a weekly basis. We have received a commission from the Lord to go and be a voice of the Lord in the house. We were appointed as shepherds and guides that instruct, fully equip, and perfect the Saints. Additionally, for the works of service and to build up the body of Christ. We will do this until we all reach oneness in the faith, knowledge of the son of God (growing spiritually), become a mature believer and reach the fullness of Christ. We know that we could do nothing without God. It's through Him that we live, move and have our very being. Through Him, we can do all things."

— Overseer Avan and Pastor Liza Chaplin

Through the Fire: Don't Stop, Drop, or Roll | 101

New Life Fellowship was another way of God assuring me that he was going to take care of me and my house as long as we served him. Pastor and First Lady of New Life Fellowship took us under their wings and taught us what a servant leader and godly example looked like. When I was not recruiting, I was obtaining coaching and mentorship in the ministry. I was able to be very transparent with the pastor. He would always address issues that I was having without me.

During that time my wife and I were trying to have a child, and we were having a lot of difficulties. We could not figure out why we could not have our second child. Pastor and the First Lady had some unmeasurable faith. They assured it was all in God's timing. What God has for you, it will come to pass. We ended up getting a dog. Lizzy was her name. Lizzy was a brown and white Chihuahua that brought much excitement to the family. When I came home, she would fight for my attention along with my wife and daughter. I was truly blessed to go back every day and have three women competing for my attention.

As you read throughout this book, you will notice that I stood clear of the word stepdad or stepfather.

Although I was not the biological father, I knew I was her father and God trusted me with that r esponsibility. The pastor taught us how to believe in something bigger than ourselves. That something is the Kingdom of God. I can recall the intense, mandatory, Friday evening meetings. The "Lead Like Jesus" impartation for leaders of the church and I was like a sponge absorbing it all. I needed those impartations, because just like I was a sponge in the church, I poured out all that I learned in the community while recruiting.

14

Formed by Fire

The Pastor at New Life Fellowship appointed me as a deacon of the church, which totally caught me off guard. I did not know what I did to deserve such a calling. I even asked God why me. I begin to remind God of my past as if he did not know.

Pastor took the time to explain, examine, and define our roles and responsibilities that we inherited. He also taught us the back side of ministry, the different processes that keep a church functioning, and dysfunctions that had to be handled in love. We learned what it took to build a church and see a vision come to pass. Time had flown by so fast. It was time for me to decide on my military career. I had to choose to convert to a full-time recruiter or reenlist and relocate. Like I mentioned earlier, being a recruiter was tough. I still had a long way to go in the Army. I did not want to spend the remainder of my time as a recruiter.

My family and I reenlisted with the option to move back to Fort Benning, Georgia. We took the assignment to go back to Fort Benning. By this time, we were a year out from PCS'ing from South Carolina back to Georgia. This time we were equipped and mature in our faith as a couple and as Christians. Before leaving South Carolina the Pastor saw fit by God to ordain me as a minister of the Gospel of Jesus Christ. All the things in life that God had trusted me with from my family, friends, job, and great leaders, he entrusted me with His word and His people. Totally unexpected, but I knew it was nonnegotiable, and the Pastor and First Lady of New Life Fellowship knew they had sewn on good ground. I never forgot they referred to my wife and me "as a precious jewel." That ministry was the cornerstone of what kept me resilient, focused, and accountable first to God, to family, and to my profession. For that, I am genuinely grateful.

It was time to move, we sold the house, said our farewells to our recruiting family and our church family, and we headed back to Georgia. We linked back up with our previous pastor from Love and Restoration. Because of our relationship, we resided at their home while we looked for a place to stay. We knew we were going to buy again and found a great realtor couple who made finding a new home comfortable. We found, bought, and closed on the second house in no time. We could not move in right away, so we headed back to our hometown to wait things out until it was time to move in our home.

I was currently on leave, but very curious about what I missed while out on recruiting. My concern was whether I could measure up to the changes. I knew I was going to stick out like a sore thumb with no combat experience. Being back at Fort Benning brought back shameful memories of not deploying with the team. I had time to figure all that out later, but this was the time to catch up with family and friends, and we did just that—picked up where we left off.

We were finally able to move into our home and get our household goods delivered. We were super excited about our home, being back in Georgia. I finally checked in to my unit, which was in the process of standing up the 11th Engineer, and I was in the Forward Support Company. The Sergeant Major interviewed me and placed me as a Platoon Sergeant. I was clueless as to all the functions that a Platoon Sergeant performed, but God had that covered as well. I had one of the best First Sergeants in the battalion, and he indeed was. He taught me everything that I needed to be successful and ensured everything I did not know or understand to research and provide him feedback. Not only was I learning something from 1SG and the other PLT Sergeant, I was also learning from the soldiers that came back from deployment. I paid close attention to some of the verbiages used. They were more than happy to share their experience. Often times, during Sergeant Time Training (STT) I would have an SGT and SPC run the lanes so that I could learn more and understand the concepts to apply.

Things were going exceptionally well on the job. I was glad to be back at Fort Benning. We attended church regularly and a big part of what was going on in the community. The Pastor and First Lady of Love and Restoration just picked us up where we left off. I became his armor bearer. An armor bearer in the religious realm helps to give strength to the pastor. They also help push the vision of the church. This was a big responsibility on top of the fifty-plus soldiers that I had. God was preparing me for what was to come.

Back at home things were well. My wife started working, my daughter was in school. We spent much of our time at parent and teacher conferences during this transition. I guess our daughter was trying to get adjusted as well, and we really did not take into consideration the effect transition had on her. We finally got things settled and had to adjust parenting styles with the understanding she was not a little girl anymore; she was coming into her own. We knew as parents to keep a clear line of communication in order to combat some of the issues and challenges that she may face.

15

Breaking Through Fire or Fear

My wife, Liya, was also going through something, I did not understand how big of a concern that something was for her. If you recall back in South Carolina we were praying, believing, and trusting God for a child. That prayer was not answered yet.

My wife wanted to give me a child. She felt as if she was not genuinely fulfilling her part as a wife. No matter how much I expressed to her that I was happy with our family, it did not make things better. I started being a little more engaged with trying to figure out what and who I needed to talk to about this issue. In South Carolina, we had seen several doctors, specialists, and tests were conducted on us both. The test results were good for us both, but the doctors were unable to diagnosis the reason we were not able to conceive in South Carolina. Now we were in Georgia seemingly going through the same thing.

Our pastor and friends at New Life Fellowship Church were praying for us; our pastors and friends at Love and Restoration were praying for us; and my wife and I were praying for each other. Can I be very transparent, at the moment I truly believe that fervent prayer of the righteous avails much and everyone that was praying I believe it reached heaven? I think that heaven was in agreement with them all. I believe the real hang-up was fear. I feared my own child coming into this world. Fear of failing them, fear of not providing for them, fear that something would happen to them, that would entirely take me out. Some would probably argue that it was selfishness as well and I would not argue back at that point.

I went before God and asked for help in that area, to lift the fear and doubt and renew in me a right spirit. I had to consult with God on this one, because I did not believe a child should cost $10,000 especially when babies were delivered every day. God spoke to me and said to me, "Son, do you know what I had to go through to send my only Begotten Son to Earth, I created and to see Him get mistreated, talked about, spit on, hung on a rugged cross, and pierced in His side? I know the feeling. Fear not, for I will be with you."

Shortly after, my wife told me she was recommended to a doctor who could help with our situation. We went to the doctor a week later, and after following the doctor's instructions, about six weeks later, my wife went back to the doctor, and the doctor confirmed that she was pregnant. We were going to have a new addition to our family. Ten months later our precious son David was born, and we were a family of five including Lizzy, the dog. Once again God came through for us. I just cannot figure out why God favored me so much, what made me different from any other person?

Meanwhile my job was doing much training and preparing to ensure the reactivation of the battalion was a success. I had the opportunity to attend several courses as a Staff Sergeant such as Senior Leader Course and Equal Opportunity Course (EO). My Senior Leader Course was located on Aberdeen Proving Ground in Maryland. The trip from Georgia to Maryland would be the longest distance that I traveled alone for a three-week course.

While driving from Maryland, my wife called me and gave me the sad news that someone had stolen Lizzy. At that time, I was about five hours from making it home. I was disturbed on the road by this report. Now I was the one who would make fun of people who would go around putting a picture of their missing pet on telephone poles. Well, the first thing I did when I got home was going around the neighborhood hanging up images of Lizzy on the telephone poles. We never got her back, and we never got another dog afterward.

The EO Course was one crucial course and would prove to be critical in the times to come. As an Equal Opportunity Leader (EOL), the course helped me focus on equal opportunity and diversity management while still assuming my Platoon Sergeant responsibilities. By this time my First Sergeant and Motor Sergeant had taught me how to prepare my record for the Sergeant First Class (SFC) board. The recruiting, preparation, and training paid off. I made the SFC list and had to make a critical decision in my life.

Before I tell you about the conclusion of the decision I had to make, let me explain what was taking place. The 11th Engineer Battalion finally reactivated. One of the horizontal engineer companies was selected to deploy. It was around the holidays, and my Sergeant Major invited my wife and me to the New Year's reception at the Colonial's house. This type of reception was usually for the Commanders, 1SG Sergeants, and their families. My wife and I were very nervous, because we had never been exposed to this form of Army tradition. We were greeted with warm welcomes upon arrival. What came next, I will always remember for the rest of my life.

The Colonial and CSM told me that they selected me to deploy with another unit, told us the month, and asked us if we accepted. Although they asked me, I knew this was their professional way of saying I was going. We gladly took the position, and they made a public announcement to the rest of the command team. Afterward, I was introduced to my new commander and 1SG.

My wife and I left the reception, and during the ride home in silence, there were no words to say, but we were filled with questions. Not only was I selected to deploy, I was called back on a ninety-day recruiter callback. The recall was a call for all Gold Badge recruiters to report back to the duty station that was directed by the Army. This initiative was to help with the recruiting efforts and to help support the war. I had to report back to Sumter, South Carolina, which was not a big problem. This gave me an opportunity to visit my church family at New Life Fellowship. It was a big concern, because it interrupted my training for my future deployment.

I completed my ninety days of recruiting. I headed back to Fort Benning to get integrated with the new company and new platoon. My sequence number came around for promotion. In order for me to get promoted, I had to reenlist indefinitely into the Army. At this point I did not understand indefinite, I thought it was forever, which caused me to doubt my decision. On November 30, 2007, I reenlisted and got promoted on the same day.

"It has and continues to be our ongoing experience that no matter what life challenges come, God's presence, provisions, and power are extended to us. His covenant commits His vast Kingdom resources to us during the storms of life so that we are not left alone. He is our secret place." — Psalms 91

— Pastors Leonard and Vanessa Backus

16

Battle Tested for Breakthrough

All my attention and focus was getting my family prepared for me to leave for fifteen-month deployment, which did not take any time at all, because Liya attended every briefing she could come to with me. The remainder of the time was given to the soldiers, my Platoon Leader who was fresh out of Basic Officer Leader Course, my Warrant Officer whom I relied on for his knowledge, and my battle buddy, SFC Milton Creed who was God sent.

The training was complete, equipment issued, health screening done, and all mandatory briefings were completed. We were placed on leave, so the next time we met it will be time to get on the plane to Iraq. I spent much time at home trying to enjoy my family, but could not help thinking about the deployment. I had to be focused and confident in the training that we had received. The theme of the church at the time was "Knowing your identity in

Christ," and also "Kingdom living," which is doing things God's way. I had to know who God said I was and not about what others say. This was God's way of saying to me that he trusted me to provide encouragement, prayer, and be an excellent example to everyone assigned to the unit.

The time had arrived for us to deploy. My family, friends, and other members from the church gathered for prayer and we were off. The message that I had to push was the Comprehensive Soldier Fitness. Although the program was not fully developed, we pushed the physical, family, emotional, spiritual, and social fundamentals. I assumed several roles in Iraq due to a shortage of personnel at the senior level. My prior position was the Platoon Sergeant. Since it was an engineering company and I was the senior construction equipment mechanic, the responsibilities of being the construction equipment supervisor were mine and also Motor Sergeant of the construction equipment. My battle SFC Creed was in charge of the Motor Pool and the wheel vehicle fleet. I still had my Equal Opportunity Leader duty as well to the company commander.

There was never an unproductive moment during those fifteen months. Later in the deployment, we received another SFC who was able to take over the Platoon Sergeant duties. He was a great addition to the team. This also freed me up to help the Forward Observe Base (FOB) with the chaplain keeping Wednesday bible study and Sunday service going during the various transitions. I made it my personal agenda when we went out on a convoy to lead each convoy in prayer, and when I was not going out on a convoy, I would get requested to lead convoy in prayer.

We did some fantastic things as a unit and were able to maintain professionally developed soldiers and place them in critical leadership positions. Somehow through all that, I was able to finish my bachelor's degree in criminal justice and my last test was proctored by my company commander. It was a four-hour test, and I think he needed that break. He was undoubtedly an engaged leader and a good one at that. I took rest and recovery leave around the tenth month of the rotation. I was the last from my platoon to take leave to ensure everyone picked the dates that were good for them.

Once I got back from vacation, I pushed the soldiers not to allow complacency to set in and to leave this place in a better condition than we found it. All the training paid off. God's hand of protection was upon us and kept us all. It was time to redeploy back to the States and that was a feeling that was unexplainable. We arrived at the airport at Fort Benning and had the warmest welcome that a soldier could receive. All of our top leadership and family members were there to celebrate our return. We knew we had some more classes to reintegrate us back with our families before we could go on leave.

Once the vacation was over, it was back to training, and once again I was placed in another unit as a Platoon Sergeant—this time in a multirole bridge company. The unit was a different setup compared to what I was accustomed to, but I knew I was equipped and had leaders to lean on who refused to let me fail.

After about a year in the company, I was approached by the CSM again about a unit that had some disciplinary issues, and he said their flag was about to get folded. Of course, nothing is a matter of option. I go where the Army sends me and wherever I go I know that God is with me. So, like a good soldier, I transferred to my fourth unit on Fort Benning. The issues the company was having were not due to soldiers' issues, but more from leaders within the unit. The situation helped me to understand roles of a Noncommissioned Officer (NCO) and Officers, and why this relationship is essential. When the Officer and NCO roles are severed, it affects the organization as a whole, and if not caught in enough time, the environment becomes toxic. I realized how much young officers relied on NCOs to square them away, and if that failed to happen, a disgruntled officer is created. His or her primary purpose for being a leader is compromised.

We were able to resolve the relationship without the flag getting folded, but not before the Army could call me up for another duty. That duty was an Advanced Individual Training Platoon Sergeant (AIT PSG), which was a relatively new initiative to replace drill sergeants at the AIT level. I could not understand how I got selected for another broadening assignment, and this time and I was not happy. I was already a Platoon Sergeant in the unit where I was located, so why did I have to go somewhere else to be a PLT SGT? I lost that decision.

I was headed to AIT PSG School, Master Resilience Training, and PCS'ing to Fort Lee, Virginia. Once again, I had to break the news to my church family. By this time we knew that sometimes our wants and desires are superseded by God's purpose and plan. The church knew very well about transition, which prepared me for the next chapter in life.

"THROUGH God, and only THROUGH God have I been able to walk the path the Lord has placed me on. It wasn't the path I had imagined or planned for, nor is it a path for the faint of heart...but one designed by God for me. Being married to a pastor for thirty-four years and ministering together with him for thirty-one years pastoring the Rock Church of Petersburg, VA, I never expected God would call him home and placed me to continue the work and ministry, standing strong for the hurting, and brokenhearted. I learned that standing in God's strength was the only acceptable position for me...relying on God to get me THROUGH each day's challenges, and they were numerous. God's strength is there for each trial, whether it's His strength in time of weakness you need, or renewed strength that comes when you are fighting, and your arms get weak from battling with the sword. God comes and gives that second wind needed. God brought me THROUGH every trial I had to face. God is so faithful! He proves His Word that you can do all things THROUGH Christ who strengthens. Depend on Him HE WILL GET YOU THROUGH."

— Reverend Sonja Davis

17

Refiners Fire

Once again, I prepared the family for transition. They were very familiar with the process by this time, which made it easier. We sold the house and conducted a recon to look for a place to reside before signing into the new duty station. We did not buy a house this time, but we signed a lease to stay in an apartment that was close to Fort Lee. During this time our daughter was in the middle of her sophomore year and our son had not started school, but was in preschool. First thing on the agenda was to get the family settled and find a church home. The only thing that I read and heard about AIT PSG duty was that I was going to be working some long hours, and I knew to take notice to the warning.

We joined a church called the Rock Church of Petersburg where we fit right in as though we had been going there for years. The Rock Church of Petersburg, Virginia, is where our family learned how to stick to it and be consistent. We applied commitment and long-suffering despite what was going on around us. We were under the care of one of God's sweetest angels. Under her teaching is where we decided when the going gets tough, we the tough (Journey family) will stay. Stay in place until God moves us. We inherited lifelong friends from heaven and mature saints. These saints had been running this race for Christ a long time, and they taught us techniques to stay in condition for our race. Our kids inherited teachers that kept them excited about God on a daily basis. It was a great time in our lives for where and what God was doing.

Now that the family was situated, church home established, it was time to sign in to my new unit. At that point, I was nervous about meeting the CSM and my 1SG. I knew the importance of impressions, and I did not want to mess it up. On the way to post, I was pulled over by the police for speeding, which now would cause me to press for time. He let me off with a warning and because I was new to the area.

Finally, I made it to the CSM office where he gave me the dos, don'ts, and the consequences if I do one of those don'ts. He also explained the benefits of all the dos the battalion had to offer. The next person who came over to pick me up was my 1SG, and that moment stuck with me throughout my career. He welcomed me to the company, told me how he was not expecting me to arrive, and referred to me as a bonus. We walked through the company, he introduced me to the team, and the rest was history.

I went home super excited about how professional things went and the motivation the young AIT soldiers demonstrated. I went on and on to my wife about my day and forgot to ask her about her day. It was hard for her to find a job, and with the long hours I worked, she was concerned that she was not relevant. I had to assure her that I considered her day and feelings before I bombarded her day with mine. Nevertheless, Liya was always eager to hear about my day. I proceeded to tell my wife my First Sergeant wanted me to attend this Sergeant Audie Murphy Board (SAMC) before he retired. He mentioned that he was retiring soon, and although he knew me a short time I exhibited qualities of this character trait.

At that point in my career, I had not disobeyed an order given by one of my superiors. I said "yes," asked who or what is the SAMC. I believe I should have asked that question before saying "yes." The 1SG guided me to the right people to get started on the journey. He retired before the next SAMC board. We received a new 1SG, and she picked up right where he left off. At the same time, we got a new CSM in as well, which was all right with me. I was familiar with change and transition by this time. This experience was also my first time hearing and getting introduced to our Regimental CSM. I was in knowledge heaven from the 1SG all the way up to the Regimental. They spent a lot of time equipping professionals, and it was evident at the rate that soldiers were getting promoted and awarded.

I wish I had time to tell you all the things I experienced at Fort Lee, but I am afraid I may miss out on recognizing all the soldiers who made me the leader that I am today. I only spent a little over a year as an AIT PSG, later got picked up on the Master Sergeant list and got frocked to 1SG. I remember sitting down talking to my 1SG about what to do, and she said, "If you have the opportunity to be a 1SG take it," and she would be there if I had any questions along the way. I prayed about it and asked God to keep me humble and keep me with a servant leader mentality. His reply was, "That is your choice." I took the First Sergeant position in the next barracks over. I served the soldiers the way all my previous 1SGs taught me. My favorite thing to say to the soldiers and leaders was, "I have the best of both worlds. I love coming to work to be around soldiers. I enjoyed more leaving work to be with my family."

God had opened up a window from heaven and honestly poured me out blessings I did not have room enough to receive. After over three years at Fort Lee I became a part of the Prestigious Audie Murphy Club, was awarded the Order of Samuel Sharpe, completed my master's degree in Divinity with a concentration in Chaplaincy, we sent our daughter off to college, and I came on orders for Korea. We were still very active in the community and the church. We had to decide whether to move as a family to Korea or go on a one-year unoccupied tour. Since our daughter was a freshman at Old Dominion University and my wife was working at the Bon Secours Washington Redskins Training Camp, we consulted with God on direction. I went to Korea on a one-year tour. At this point in my career, things seemed to line up. I was eager to see what came next.

"We have learned that everything is better and purer if we run it through God. It is like running air or water through a purifier; they always come out better on the other side. Many times we will think that something is a good idea, but when we run it through God, it becomes even better. When we take time to have the mind of Christ and look to His Word to filter through those ideas, He can divinely enlighten, inspire, direct, guide and instruct us. It's like having the Master Author, Editor, and Publisher, who knows how to tailor our decisions to His will. The word through implies that there is a beginning and an ending that by definition can only be accessed, 'by means of,' 'by way of,' or 'by the agency of' something. Colossians 1:16a says, 'For by Him were all things created.' Verse 17b states, 'and by Him, all things consist.' John 1:3a reiterates, 'All things were created by Him.' We have come to know that all of our blessings (such as healing, deliverance, financial needs, joy, wisdom, forgiveness, and every good and perfect gift) come by the agency of/through God."

— Pastor Fredrick and Mrs. Vera Brown

18

Don't Forget to Say Thanks

It was off to South Korea with a possible choice of duty station upon completion. No matter how strong I am in my faith and how often I am away from my family, I have learned never to get comfortable or used to being away from home.

One thing my family does is an excellent job in reception and integration of each other back into the fold. I was in for a great big surprise when I arrived in Korea. The only time I had ever been overseas was by way of deployment, and that was enough excitement to last me a lifetime. The integration and culture awareness was a critical piece to my success in Korea and would also help shape my drive toward accomplishing every mission.

One thing I remembered throughout basic training and my career was to have a battle buddy. At this point in my life, battle buddies was more than just a person who goes everywhere with you. The battle buddy I was looking for was someone that I could be accountable to, and they did not mind being responsible for as well. One who was transparent, a go-getter, and a standard bearer in their home and profession. The Lord answered my prayer with not just one but two battle buddies in Mike and Rich. We ended up being in the same battalion 2-1 Air Defense Artillery. We were inseparable, held each other accountable, and importantly we kept each other and our families lifted up in prayer. This battle buddy relationship was established within two weeks of us being in the country.

Next on the agenda was to find out what position I was going to be in. As soon as I arrived, the CSM welcomed us with a smile and told us what the commander priorities were and where she needed help in those areas. She took our Master Sergeant rank off and put the diamond back on. She began to show us around the footprint of the battalion. She also introduced us to the people we were going to change responsibility with. Most of the battalion had Sergeant First Class positions. The leader whose position I was going to assume was quickly approaching his Estimated Return from Overseas (DEROS) date.

For the CSM we were right on time and we got to work immediately to get the list of things our leaders wanted to accomplish. Our Warrant Officer battle buddy was working on the staff. He was our eyes in the skies and ensured that we were in the know. I was introduced to the company commander and received my counseling. My commander got his priority from the Battalion Commander. Afterward, I was out in the area introducing myself to the soldiers. It took them some time to get used to me always being around guiding, coaching, mentoring, correcting, and leading. The soldiers had the uncut version of what an engaged leader looked like, and they challenged me every day to live up to the standard and keep them accountable to the rule.

As a unit, we accomplished things that they never achieved before. We have gotten through adversity and challenges and made some question their existence for being in the military. We were confident in the resiliency of the soldiers in our unit. The best foundation we were able to establish was our Family Readiness Group (FRG) program. Hands down we had the best programmers in the entire peninsula. I believe we had cracked the code on that. Our FRG leader was able to help the commander team establish a foundation quickly.

Cannot Thank You Enough

Lord for thirty-six years I have tried to find ways to say Thank You and express my gratitude.
I know often I disappointed you with my lack of faith, disobedience, and not to mention my attitude.
I used to believe that to make it to heaven depended solely on my good works and deeds.
Lord, Thank YOU for taking me back to the place where I first believed.
Lord, do you remember the time I spent in the hospital due to asthma attacks and constant shortness of breath. Of course you do, you were the one who told me the outcome would not be death.
What about those times we spent with the lights and water off, no food in the home to eat? Through it all, I watched my grandma still worship at your feet.
So how can I say thanks for things you have done. Mainly my first thought of becoming a Christian was "there goes my fun."
Lord, what was the purpose of my sisters and me spending time in foster homes? Was it a test of our faith to prove through it all you were there and never left us alone?
While reading November 4 daily bread, the author Bill Crowder said: "Our God is deeply concerned about what concerns us." Lord, did I ever Thank

YOU for breaking those generation habits and curses?
Lord, what about that time I got caught breaking the law? Six-month probation for throwing a rock and breaking a window out of a car.
As we strive to reach new heights, go from faith to faith, and glory to glory, I often ponder about leaving a legacy and how will my children tell YOUR story.
The Story about the one (GOD), who sent the one son (JESUS), and the one son who sent the comforter (HOLY SPIRIT) to guide us into all truth.
Thank YOU for my beginning, saving a wretch like me and pursuing me in my youth.
My one desire is to give you my all. I am praying each day my all is my best. Through my best your grace and love will manifest.

Is it humanly possible to show how truly thankful we are for your act of valor on the cross? Still, to this day no one can calculate that cost.
Lord, I know I am in your will, and you gave me a purpose and plan. My intention, desire, life, and wants I place all in your hand.
So, as I pursue a close relationship with you and discover our secret place, let every thought, deed, act to include my worship put a smile on your face.

Out of all the poems I have written, this is the one
I don't want to end. The reason is that you have
certainly been a true friend.
Thank YOU for my kids, family, and friends as I
press toward the mark and forgetting those things
in the past. I especially appreciate you for my wife
LeTasha, my better half.
Satan I serve you notice, you should have taken me
out when you had a chance. Now I am a gatekeeper
of God's kingdom, watching his people advance.
Yes, many are called, few chosen. The harvest is
plentiful, but the laborers are few. Lord, my
THANKS is to You for carrying me through.

The next thing on my agenda was to find a place of worship. Although I had my battle buddies and my unit, I could not forget my calling. I started attending church on-post. I stayed off the military installation in a three-bedroom apartment, and every day coming and going to work and church, I would pass this other church. One day I decided to visit the church. The name of the church was New Testament Christian Church, and, man, was I in for a treat. The Pastor and First Lady of the church were the priceless gem that God placed in Korea waiting for me to behold.

Over time we developed a relationship that only God knew how to orchestrate. He was a retired First Sergeant, but more importantly, he had a passion for people that could not be taught nor could it be copied. He had to be God-given and only developed through knowing and hearing the heart of God. I became an apprentice under him on how to take the Word of God and not just talk it, but live it in my everyday walk. This type of leadership style helped me quickly rehabilitate soldiers and get them back on the right track before they jeopardized their entire career. I was able to do it the doctrinal way and more importantly God's way.

The New Testament Christian Church provided a place where soldiers could fellowship and not subject themselves to activities that would have a negative impact on their careers. I went home halfway through my tour in Korea to ensure that I kept the fire in my marriage burning and relationship with my family current. I returned to finish my journey, but not before the seed was planted about writing a book.

There was a young man who served with me in Korea. He spent his time walking up hill 303, and when he reached the top, he would pray and write.

He later wrote a book called *The Climb*, and he encouraged others around him to write a book. The seed was planted, but it was watered with doubt, fear, and excuses on my part. About a year after I left Korea I received an email from the Pastor in Korea. He told me he just finished writing a book titled Important Step. The book was retiling the ground and more seeds being replanted. If I was not at work, I was serving in the church or community with the SAMC. Time flew by so fast that I felt there was more I had to accomplish. I established lifelong friends and met a great leader who willingly shared knowledge with soldiers and me. Our mutual friendship that was established confirmed we would follow each other through any conflicts. My year was up, and my DEROS was approaching and it was time to say my sad farewells. I must say I shared some Hallmark moments in Korea.

We ended up getting an assignment to Fort Stewart, Georgia. The family was excited to be heading back to the south, to jump on the Marne Train at Fort Stewart, Georgia. Our daughter would remain in Virginia to finish up her degree as we transitioned. At that moment, I was at eighteen years in my military career, and twenty always seemed to be the unspoken mark to transition out of the Army. My family and I had some decisions to make.

We never set goals as a rank, position, or place in the Army. I practically just went where my leader told me, trusted where the Army sent me, and knew God covered us. If they told me to go to a board, I went, to a position I went, and to war I went. Throughout that time, I never doubted the training and leadership that God had placed around me. I merely did my duty with compassion, never out of compulsion or reluctance. I took joy serving in the United States Army, serving soldiers and their families, and the people of the United States of America.

More importantly I loved my family. It was important for me to give my family the same energy, compassion, and guidance that was given to the senior leaders, peers, and subordinates alike. It always concerned me when I saw people trying to elude bringing a balance to their family and profession. I have learned that balance is critical toward maintaining unity within military families. At this point in my career, we were planning a transition out of the Army. God had other plans in mind and people who would assist with His plan.

19

Promise Keeper: No Scorches or Burns

I returned from Korea and back to Virginia to pick the family up as we were headed to Fort Stewart, Georgia. The transition was a little more relaxed because we were in Georgia, but we were unfamiliar with the Fort Stewart area.

Like always we reconned the area, stayed in the on-post hotel, got ourselves used to the city, and looked for a home to rent. By this time, we agreed that we were not going to buy another house until we were sure on our final destination. We finally found the perfect place to stay that was close to my job, my wife's future job, and to our son's school. I did not take as much leave as I usually would after taking midtour leave while in Korea. I signed in from vacation and went through an expedited in-processing due to my rank. They assigned me to 2nd Infantry Brigade Combat Team, 703rd Brigade

Support Battalion attached to 3-7th Infinity Battalion, Hotel Company Forward Support Company.

Yes, it confused me at first, but I had to learn this environment quickly, due to the long history of 3rd Infantry Division, and the pace that I heard concerning Marne Train move in. Once I met the CSM for the 703rd BSB, I was handed over to a CSM who was there temporarily until another CSM arrived. They both gave me their expectations and tasks that I needed to focus my attention on. The leader in the company moved to a different company within the battalion and I assumed responsibilities for that area.

I had my counseling with the commander, and he knew exactly what he wanted to be fixed, things he wanted to be sustained, and he instantly trusted that I would get those tasks accomplished. I did not want to disappoint him, my family, or the team. Once again, I committed myself to providing the things that all soldiers in the Army are entitled to and that is outstanding leadership. Now the fun would begin.

When I signed in the company, I was already scheduled for back-to-back local Field Training Exercises. Those exercises were in preparation for three consecutive Combat Training Center Rotation (CTC), the first one was at Fort Polk, Louisiana, for thirty days. About a month later we were heading to Fort Bliss, Texas, for thirty more days. The third one was in Fort Irwin, California, at the National Training Center. Each CTC we attended, we progressively got better on every area of our skills and craft. We were considered the most highly trained unit on Fort Stewart at that time and were ready at any moment for the call.

The neat thing about all that training was there was very little complaining from the soldiers and their families. We kept them in the know on things. We ensured the families the training was essential for their loved ones staying alive on the battlefield. One of my primary objectives was to give my trust to the soldiers and their family members and allow them to receive or reject my trust. Once they receive that trust, I cautioned them that it was fragile and not to break it. For those that did not accept it, I had to find out why. I knew it was due to previous leadership or they were not a team player. My trust was geared toward meeting the commander intent and to insure that soldiers progressed, not remain stagnant, and committed to the Army. Once the confidence was established, there was not any place I could take them where they did not receive favorable and above standard results.

During the second CTC rotation to Fort Bliss, Texas, I met one of the CSMs, whom we were there to support. He asked me how long I had been in the Army and how many times I had been looked at for the Sergeant Major list. I replied with eighteen years and I was getting out at twenty. He asked me how many people got picked up for SGM list this year. My reply was one Sergeant Major. He paused a moment and told me not to get out while the Army was not promoting. For some reason, he was sure that I was going to make SGM.

At that same moment, my mind flashed back to Korea and a young soldier who had asked me a similar question and I gave him the same reply I gave the SGM. The soldier's response was totally different when I told him I was getting out and heading to "fort living room on camp couch." The soldier's reply was, "You are what makes the Army bad." For a moment I was about to get offended until he explained himself.

He said, "The Army has invested a lot in you and it shows by the way you treat people. Now you are going to turn and leave the Army with all that knowledge when you still have more in you."

I took those two moments and tucked them close to heart. I knew I would need it for a later decision-making point in my life. After all the training exercises, we finally caught a break. Prior to all the training, my wife had visited several churches in an effort to find a church home. We had visited several churches in the area but none that we agreed upon.

"Sometimes life hits you with the unexpected. Our son was born with a congenital heart disease known as pulmonary atresia. At birth, his pulmonary valve did not open, thereby preventing blood from flowing to his lungs. As a result, his body was deprived of oxygenated blood. At one day old, he underwent open-heart surgery. For the next fourteen years, he lived and functioned as an ordinary growing boy. In March of 2015 while at a regular biannual checkup, his cardiologist decided that it was time for intervention, meaning that he needed another open-heart surgery to give him an artificial pulmonary valve. Needless to say, he was devastated, and as parents, we were concerned. No one wants their teenager to be opened up on the table, have their heart stopped and then revived. These are the moments that you decide

what you really believe. Do you walk in faith or do you give in to the fear of what-if? We decided to walk in faith because we knew that through God Luke would be fine. He went in for surgery on Tuesday morning, and even after a slight complication with his breathing tube post-surgery, by Thursday at lunch we were leaving the hospital, straight out of ICU, to go home! What we thought would be a long, drawn-out recovery at the hospital turned into a quick visit to give Luke a fully functioning heart. We do not doubt that God has a great plan for our son's life and that through Him, all things are possible for Luke."

— Pastor Aaron and Kristi Cowart

We finally visited Live Oak Church, a place where we continued to grow as a family. Pastor and First Lady Cowart at Live Oak Church were the example God used to continually propel our family in our faith walk. It was as if God had purposely set them in Hinesville, Georgia, just for us. While at Live Oak Church (LOC) we immediately went to work in the church and the community.

While attending LOC I was selected along with three others to attend one seminar in Atlanta called Celebrate Recovery. Celebrate Recovery simply explained is a recovery program. This program is geared to target all "hurts, habits, and hang-ups." This is by no means limited to behavior that is compulsive, high anxiety, sex, drug, and alcohol addictions, and eating disorders just to name a few. In the beginning, I thought I was going to get training to help others, but God had a plan in store for me through the CR program.

Once we arrived from Atlanta the group leader advised us on the next step in order to get the CR program off the ground. The next step was almost a year long, 12-step study with eight principles based off the Beatitude of the Bible in Matthew 5: 3–10. This was the pause in my life that I needed in order to do a self-evaluation and deal with some issues that had lain dormant. This program made me a more transparent leader and gave me the ability to look beyond people's past mistakes and failures. The program assisted me with the skills I needed to help individuals become successful and make the program a success at my local church. God was really equipping me for the things to come and preparing me for His plan and purpose. Once we completed the required training, we opened it up to the community, which was a blessing.

"As we reflect on our lives, we can visibly see many moments where there was no doubt that God was orchestrating and ordering our steps. We can recall the moment when God spoke as it relates to planting a new church in El Paso. Birthing a ministry was something we never thought we would be doing, but so glad we did. We know that it is God's direction that makes it possible to navigate through life's transitions because this was an assignment that we knew we couldn't handle alone and had to trust God completely for guidance. Over the past several years we witnessed many lives changed for the greater, negative reports reversed, and families mended, just to share a few. This we believe is a direct result of God's goodness and our faith to believe that through God nothing is impossible. We believe even more now that to get 'to,' you have to go 'through.'"

— Pastors Eric and Yaisa Hallback

20

Not Yet...
Just Getting Started

Meanwhile, it was time to decide as to whether or not we were going to stay in the military past twenty years. It was not the hardest decision I had to make in life. As a matter of fact it would be one of the easiest.

I remember having a conversation with my last Battalion Commander who gave me some sound advice. He said, "God has taken care of you and your family this far, how can you get this far and doubt Him now." Shortly after this conversation my wife woke up in the middle of the night and told me that the Lord said, "I was going to get promoted on the next list and what are your plans?" I told her I was going to continue the journey, and she was in agreement.

Make no mistake about it, if she was not in my corner I would not have extended this mission.

I was thrilled and relieved at the fact she was still excited about continuing this military journey with me. The promotion list came out and God placed my name on the list. God placed me on a ten-month journey that would fine-tune my developmental process. Just like all the other transitions, my wife and I prayed and decided what was best for our family. We decided it was best I travel to the next phase alone and seek the Lord's guidance on the next phase of this journey.

The plan consisted of me attending school on my own, after graduation from (USASMA), we would revisit the Lord to see what was next on His agenda for the Journey family. I arrived at the new place to complete school, but not only school, to a place where the ground in which this book would be planted is fertile, with the promise of fruits to be brought forth. It was imperative that I got under a spiritual covering, not so much for the sake of sin. This time it was about the anointing that was upon my life and protecting that anointing. The anointing is "to authorize, or set apart, a person for a particular work or service"

If God was going to continue to be the head of my life, I had to protect my life. God has set me apart for a particular work or service and that work was assigned to me. While on this journey I had a facilitator that encouraged the students to write and not allow fear to stop us. It appeared to be elementary to tell someone at this age something so simple. As simple as it may have seemed, it worked. After the facilitator dropped that encouragement in my spirit, it erased doubts concerning writing.

I was led to Rock Faith Center with a very special Pastor and First Lady. I was placed under his care until God gave me my follow-on instructions. When it comes down to Shepard and Discipleship, the Pastor at Rock Faith Center had a personal encounter with God. His intelligence quotient (IQ) for the Kingdom of God and perfecting the Saints was downloaded to him straight from heaven. He had challenged all disciples/sheep in his flock to pick up their cross and stop walking over it. Finally, the time had come, the season was here. God's voice was clear, and he said to write. God had ensured me that he had spared my life so that others' lives could be saved. Like Moses, I started coming up with all kinds of excuses why this task was too big, or how my writing skills were not the best. I had no clue how to complete the work after I was done writing.

Through a series of events and people, I was shown when God tells you to do something, He has already aligned the right people and resources to ensure His task through you is completed. God began to lay certain people on my heart, and then he directed others in my path. Once people were aligned, God added the one thing that He'd been providing for me from the start: favor. God's instructions were clear, and the time span he gave was limited. This was going to require total commitment and concentration.

Procrastination was not allowed and there were no other chances to step out on this window of opportunity. When I started, an artist came to mind when I was coming up with my book design. I contacted him, gave him a scripture, and he immediately began brainstorming on the book cover. After minutes of brainstorming, he came up with an idea for the design of the book. He advised me on getting a graphic designer to ensure that the cover was professional and not cartoonish. We agreed that he would hold the idea until a graphic designer was found, and I was going to carry on with the writing of the book.

Some doubt started to creep in, but I was quickly reminded by my wife to do what God told me to do, and that was to write. While in school the Holy Spirit brought to my remembrance of a photographer in the classroom. I was prompted to ask him if he knew a graphic designer, and he said yes. The photographer typed up a text, showed me the information that he was going to send to the guy he knew. He sent the text out on Wednesday afternoon. Thursday came around and I was wondering to myself if he heard anything from the graphic designer. I did not want to seem impatient, so I waited until the end of the day and asked him. The graphic designer did answer back and gave the photographer the approval for me to contact him. I was kind of nervous and reluctant so I asked, "Did this person have a website?" The photographer responded back stating, "You will have to call him and ask."

That evening I gave the graphic designer a call. We did our introduction, built a little trust, and got down to the reason for my request. He gave me his website, and I reviewed the information on his website. I was pleased with what I saw. I got permission from the graphic designer to put him on a conference call with the artist. I had considered the artist the gatekeeper to my idea for the cover. The graphic designer agreed to the conference call. The artist and the graphic designer begin to talk their professional language to one another. Within twenty minutes of back and forth brainstorming, the graphic designer created a design over the phone and sent it to my email. I was left speechless when I reviewed the book cover and instantly began to give God to praise.

The graphic designer educated me on the road ahead and everything that would be required to complete the book from start to finish. He was such a blessing, I begin to question God about whether this was real or not with the favor, instruction, and the pace things were moving. I linked my wife in on the conversation with the graphic designer so that I could stay focused on my assignment to write. I begin to show my gratitude by thanking him for assisting me with my first book. He asked one thing of me, and that is that I stop calling it my first book and call it my last book. He explained that everything I do should feel like my last book, so put your all into it.

Things were finally getting started. I had to iron out some military and legal concerns. God led me to talk with another classmate in the class. He gave me some sound advice and led me to an instructor who taught at the academy and who also used to work in Washington, DC, with public affairs. I linked in with her and explained my vision. She guided me to the right person, and he gave me the information I needed to stay in compliance with the military.

God knew what I needed to accomplish my last book and He supplied all my needs according to His riches and glory in Christ Jesus. I knew God was only giving me a specific time that he would hold this window from heaven open to complete this project. It was also clear that he did not want it to interfere with the schoolwork and my purpose in the current environment. I put forth everything into this project and allowed God to guide my thoughts. I was constantly praying to God that I achieve His intent and complete this during the season God allotted. The blessing, favor, and anointing was ever present in my life. The Holy Spirit was leading and guiding me in all truth. There were times when I did not feel worthy, but God's presence in my life made it worthy.

Conclusion

Throughout life's trials and tribulations, I have gained a wealth of wisdom and knowledge. I owe a great big thank you to my friend of twenty-five years and wife of sixteen years to Mrs. Aaliya Journey. The experience of being a proud father was gained with our two children who are madly in love with us. I am a proud son, loving brother, cool cousin, uncle, grandson, and nephew. More importantly I am a child of The Most High God, a man of God, a servant leader or a leader that is serving. I would not be who I am without the love and support of my family, friends, ministry leaders, and military mentors.

I have had and currently have the privilege and honor to serve the best Army, the best profession in this Profession of Arms, the greatest Nation in the world and no one is telling me to stop.

One of the most significant experiences that I have gained and shared with others is the love of Jesus Christ. For Jesus is why I do what I do and won't stop. Christ has directed people in my path for a purpose and plan, to fulfill His promise for my life. The events that occurred in my life were the lessons I had to learn. I would not trade those lessons for anything in the world. I won't stop until I reach my destination: HEAVEN. God created everything, and out of all the things God created, He saw fit in Genesis 1:26 to gather together Jesus and the Holy Spirit and say, "Let us make man in our image, after our likeness." God took it a step further to give us dominion, then he blessed us. That blessing gave us access to heaven to back us up for the task that comes next. Then God said, "Be fruitful and multiply, and replenish the earth, and subdue it."

Life as we knew it was good, then it went terribly wrong in the garden, everything was out of order. The order of God's image and likeness on our life, the blessing that gave us access to heaven to back us up, and to be fruitful, multiply, replenish and subdue the earth was stripped away. The only way to get that relationship back would be at an extremely expensive price. It had to be brought back. That was not the only thing that was taken away. Our lives were taken away. No one else could bring forth balance except that one who created it all.

John 3:16 describes why God would send His only begotten son to save us, and that was because of the Love for the world and everything in it. While seeing insignificant me still sinning, God demonstrated His love toward me through Christ's death, His blood repurchased me to live. Although I could not, did not, and even tried to understand what that love looked like, God was still looking beyond our faults and finding a need. I was looking for love in material things, relationship, family, money, and occupation. I would always come up short and missed the mark on love in those places. It was not until I accepted Jesus as my Lord and Savior, gained a personal relationship with Him that true love would be revealed.

Through that true love is where I can look back and see all things that God has brought me through. Even those things that I knew I should not have lived through, God was committed to getting the glory out of my life. God's love for me through His son Jesus Christ matured and taught me how to utilize the power of the Holy Spirit, how to break through with the power of the Holy Spirit. Every trial, tribulation, hurt, habit, and hang-up in my life no longer held me captive. I learned that everything that happened in my life had to be approved by

God, because through God all things are possible, and I can do all things through Christ who gives me strength.

God promises me that all the waters that I had to pass through in my life, despite the condition of the water, He would be with me. He also promised me the river's route that I had to travel would not overtake me whether with the current or against the current…keep moving. Then he reminded me when I walked through fires of fear, doubt, rejection, testing, and proving comes my way it will not scorch me. In other words, I will not look like any of the things that I went through except the image and likeness of God.

God promises me after I pass through the fire, the flame coming from the fire won't burn me. God was telling me that even my past won't have any effect on my future. Romans 8:18 says, "For I reckon that the suffering of this present time is not worthy to be compared with the glory which shall be revealed in us." May I add the suffering of my past and present time is not worthy to be compared with the glory which shall be revealed in us.

God, thank you for allowing me to know you in the power of your resurrection and the fellowship of your suffering. Thank you, heavenly Father, for purchasing me, bringing me through, and giving me the ability to break through. Thanks for permitting me to write my last book. I pray it brings you Glory.

Acknowledgments

While I was sitting in class one morning, the Lord spoke to me and said, "Write." I knew exactly what he wanted me to write about; this story has been brewing for years.

But fear fell heavily upon me. I begin to make excuses as to why I could not write, the tasks I had to accomplish, and the time that it would take to accomplish what was already set before me. All that day I waited for an answer back from God to confirm if he had the right person or was I supposed to deliver that message to someone else. By lunchtime that day, I did not hear back from the Lord. So I sent up excuses telling God that I was not a very good writer. I did not know the proper steps of writing a book or whom to contact to start the process. I had excuses after excuses, such as not knowing any editors, publishers, or graphic designers.

That evening I shared with my wife what the Lord told me to do, and afterward I started to write. Day after day for about fifteen days straight I would come home after school and write about 1,500 words of what the Lord dropped in my spirit. During those times of writing I would get discouraged and come up with the same excuses and more to my wife.

My wife would simply say, "What did God tell you to do?" Those words alone spoke value and relinquished all excuses and doubt. Through my obedience to God's voice, God provided me with an outstanding publisher and graphic designer (Tony) of Malkia Publishing, whom I have grown fond of. The gatekeeper of the idea for my book cover the artist (TJ). As a bonus and special favor from God he sent us Sandy, my editor.

A sincere thanks to the staff and faculty of the United States Sergeant Major Academy (USASMA) and my classmates of Class 68 "By Example."

This would not have been possible without the love and support from my wife, LeTasha. LeTasha is my motivation, the coach in my corner, the protector of my interest, and buffer from distraction as I fulfilled the Lord's command. Special thanks to our daughter, Shadalia, and son, Jeriden. I cannot wait to see their expression once they read the book.

Acknowledgments

To all my family, pastors, and friends who contributed to this book, I thank you all so much for your prayer and impartation. If I failed to mention your name, I am sure you fall in the family and friends category—please charge it to the mind not the heart.

To my Lord and Savior, I pray this brings you joy, puts a smile on your face, but most importantly brings you Glory!

About the Author

Jimmy Rush is a native of Albany, Georgia, and comes from a family of six: grandmother Carrie B, mother Lydia L, and three sisters: Shaleta, Carrie S, and Lydia S. He is the husband, friend, and lover to LeTasha Rush, and proud father of Shadalia and Jeriden. He has been a Christian for twenty years and accepted his call to ministry shortly after receiving his salvation.

Jimmy's primary redemptive gifts are Giving, Faith, and Mercy. He's motivated to share the love of God with all who will hear it and by his life example. He seeks to nurture and develop those around him in the fear of the Lord and life of love that we are all called to walk in. Jimmy firmly believes that ministry must begin at home to wife and children. Further, he seeks to walk in submission to God first and then the shepherd whom God has placed him under. Jimmy desires to serve God through worship, prayer, teaching, and encouraging others.

Jimmy is serving his twentieth year on active duty in the United States Army. His ministry gifts are teaching, preaching, and counseling. He has an associate degree in Business and bachelor's degree in Criminal Justice both from Troy State University and a master's degree in Divinity with a concentration in Chaplaincy from Liberty University.

Jimmy's purpose is to remain a multifunctional, usable servant of God and to be the living breathing manifestation of God's Glory. He enjoys spending time with his family.

www.ingramcontent.com/pod-product-compliance
Lightning Source LLC
Chambersburg PA
CBHW032040290426
44110CB00012B/883